Storybook Costumes for Dolls

Patterns and Design Techniques

First edition/First printing

To purchase additional copies of this book, please contact: Reverie Publishing Company,
130 South Wineow Street, Cumberland, Maryland 21502. 888-721-4999. www.reveriepublishing.com

Library of Congress Control Number 2009923600

ISBN: 978-1-932485-56-1

Project Editor: Krystyna Poray Goddu
Design: Lynn Amos

Front cover: Little Bo Peep - Tuesday's Child by Boneka; Little Red Riding Hood - Little Darling by The Doll Studio; Heidi - Tulah by Kish & Company; Alice in Wonderland - Bridget by Dianna Effner Porcelain Dolls Back cover: Snow White - Leeann by Affordable Designs; Juliet - Vintage Ginny by The Vogue Doll Company from the collection of Delene Budd

Printed and bound in Korea

Storybook Costumes for Dolls

Patterns and Design Techniques

Londie Phillips

Reverie

PUBLISHING COMPANY

Acknowledgements

Thank you to everyone who has contributed in some way to the making of this book.

Thank you to the dollmakers for lending their wonderful dolls to model these storybook designs: Helen Kish of Kish & Company for Riley and Tulah; Delene Budd, co-owner of the Nancy Ann Storybook Doll Company, for lending her vintage Muffy and vintage Ginny®; Linda Smith, president of The Vogue Doll Company, for Ginny; Rosemarie Ionker of Boneka for Tuesday's Child; Denis Bastien, designer/ owner of Affordable Designs, for Leeann; and Dianna Effner for the many characters from Expressions and her one-of-kind portfolio, including: Bridget, Allison, Nicole, Little Lou and Little Lou II, June, Gina and Wednesday's Child, and also for Little Darling, The Doll Studio. I am so grateful to have the opportunity to work with such beautiful dolls and their makers.

Thank you to the designers who have lent their words of experience, all wonderful artists who inspire me and others to stretch and grow in our craft.

Thank you to Scott Gustafson for his gracious lending of "Little Bo Peep," from *Favorite Nursery Rhymes from Mother Goose*, 2007.

Thank you to Timothy Hoover, owner of Top Stitch, a sewing machine wonderland.

Thank you to the countless dedicated people involved with Wikipedia and Wikimedia Commons and Project Gutenberg for bringing volumes of information to our fingertips.

Thank you, Krystyna Poray Goddu and Thomas Farrell, of Reverie Publishing, for having the vision for this project and for all of your help along the way. Thank you to Lynn Amos for the lovely graphics and book design.

And finally, and especially, thank you to my family and friends who have indulged me with time, conversation and encouragement. Thank you, Dennis, for your love and generosity that has allowed me to pursue my dreams, I love you; thank you, Hollie and Xavier Venegas, for lending daily insight, wisdom and high-fives, you are great! Thank you, Debbie Battjes and Lola for driving me around San Francisco on fabric quests and Debbie Myers for library help; and hugs to Georgie Girl, our sweet yellow lab, my constant sewing room companion.

Dedicated

in loving memory

to the one who taught me to sew

Hazelann Parker

my ♥ mom

Preface

It was in the early 1960s that I picked up my first sewing needle; I was about nine years old and Barbie had made her debut. My best friend, Suzanne Waggoner, had a wonderful collection of Barbie fashions and together we would play for hours. When I asked my mom for additional clothes for *my* bubble-cut Barbie, whose entire wardrobe consisted of the black-and-white striped swimsuit and the high heels she came in, I was handed a threaded needle and a small piece of pale-green cotton print. Somehow I knew the needle would supplant trips to the toy store for doll clothes, but it was then that my love for sewing, fabrics and fashion design began. Playing with and dressing dolls became secondary to what fashion I could stitch next. I soon graduated to using the sewing machine and commercial patterns, but nothing thrilled me so much as when my mom offered me the fabric from her lavender formal (seen on the dedication photo) so that I could make a Barbie gown.

As little girls do, I put away the dolls when I entered junior high school, but I began stitching my own clothes and eventually prom dresses and wedding gowns for family and friends. At eighteen, I moved to San Francisco to study fashion design and learned the intriguing art of pattern drafting. While the skills I learned there took me many places, it was nearly twenty years before I would rediscover dolls.

Carolyn Arnold, an avid doll collector and friend, invited me to attend a doll show. It was a research adventure for me; I had boxes of wedding-gown and theatrical-costume remnants and I thought I might parlay them into doll clothes for a Christmas boutique. To my surprise, I found collectible dolls fascinating. I soon began to freelance for Ashton-Drake Galleries, and my latent love for designing doll clothes re-emerged.

Through much encouragement from Dianna Effner, a dear friend and celebrated pioneer in doll crafting, I have now come to write this pattern book. Through this process, the LORD has truly given me the desires of my heart. I hope my years of joy working with dolls and the many wonderful people in the doll industry will somehow spill out onto your sewing table—and if this happens, be sure to share that joy with a young friend.

Contents

The Models

Following is a list of the dolls that model the costumes in chapters 2, 3 and 4.

Chapter 2: Classic and Endearing

Page 26
Leeann, 11 inches, by Affordable Designs
Vintage Muffy, 8 inches, by Nancy Ann Storybook
    Dolls, Inc.

Page 27
Tuesday's Child, 10 inches, by Boneka
Alice, 12 inches, by Dianna Effner Porcelain Dolls

Page 28
Allison, 11 inches, molds by Expressions
Riley, 7½ inches, by Kish & Company

Page 29
Riley, 7½ inches, by Kish & Company
Bridget, 11 inches, molds by Expressions

Page 30
Ginny, 8 inches, by The Vogue Doll Company
Leeann, 11 inches, by Affordable Designs

Page 31
Tuesday's Child, 10 inches, by Boneka
Gina, 12 inches, molds by Expressions

Page 32
Tuesday's Child, 10 inches, by Boneka
Vintage Ginny, 8 inches, by The Vogue Doll
    Company

Chapter 3: Old-World Elegance and Charm

Page 33
Tuesday's Child, 10 inches, by Boneka
Little Darling, 13 inches, by The Doll Studio

Page 34
Riley, 7½ inches, by Kish & Company
Bridget, 11 inches, molds by Expressions

Page 35
Tuesday's Child, 10 inches, by Boneka

Page 36
Little Lou, 11 inches, by Dianna Effner Porcelain
    Dolls
Little Red Riding Hood, 11 inches, by Dianna
    Effner Porcelain Dolls

Page 37
Little Lou II, 11 inches, molds by Expressions
Leeann, 11 inches, by Affordable Designs

Chapter 4: Twenty-First-Century Avant Garde

Page 39
Tulah, 8 inches, by Kish & Company
Alice, 11 inches, by Dianna Effner Porcelain Dolls

Page 40
Bridget, 12 inches, molds by Expressions
Nicole, 12 inches, molds by Expressions

Page 41
Bridget, 12 inches, molds by Expressions
Tuesday's Child, 10 inches, by Boneka

Page 42
Little Darling, 13 inches, by The Doll Studio
Ginny, 8 inches, by The Vogue Doll Company

Page 43
Nicole, 12 inches, molds by Expressions

Introduction

> "The grandmother had a lot of pretty dolls, and she showed Heidi how to make dresses and pinafores for them, so that Heidi learnt how to sew…"
>
> —*Heidi*, Johanna Spyri

We love our dolls and we love storybook characters. Both transport us to realms in our imaginations that inspire dreams, and invite us to ponder and explore the innocence of childhood and the lessons learned there. Together they lend a tangible experience to pretend and play.

The patterns in this book have been created to embrace your imagination and develop your skills. Three different design categories, Classic, Old World and Twenty-First-Century Avant Garde, allow you to choose a rendition and/or a skill level for creating costumes for eight storybook characters. The Classic designs represent common costume renditions, utilizing easy-to-find fabrics and trims. Old World designs include more attention to detail and are slightly more complex; the use of silks and finer fabrics and trims gives them a portrait or heirloom quality. The Twenty-First-Century Avant Garde patterns are whimsical; some creative license has been taken with the costume designs. These are the most imaginative and perhaps most interesting, but simplified

sewing techniques and step-by-step details provide hours of opportunity for design and sewing success. Before you begin, please study the sewing tips and constructions details in Part II: Helpful Tips and General Instructions.

Patterns are included for the Real Princess, Alice in Wonderland, Little Bo Peep, the Sugar Plum Fairy, Snow White, Little Red Riding Hood, Heidi and Shakespeare's Juliet. They can be made to fit four sizes of dolls ranging from 7½ to 12 inches high. The finished fashions are modeled by Riley and Tulah from Kish & Company; Ginny from The Vogue Doll Company; vintage Muffy from Nancy Ann Storybook Doll Company; Tuesday's Child from Boneka; Dianna Effner Originals from Dianna Effner Porcelain Dolls; Leeann from Affordable Designs; Dianna Effner Dolls, molds by Expressions and Little Darling from The Doll Studio. These eight storybook characters have distinctive styles, yet with small adaptations, the patterns can be used to create virtually any character you choose.

It is time to begin your costuming adventure; you never know where the story will lead.

Part I: The Storybook Characters and

Chapter 1

The Characters

The Princess and the Pea, illustration by A. J. Ford, 1894

The Princess and the Pea, illustration by Edmund Dulac, 1911

> "...she was in a terrible state from the rain and storm. The water streamed out of her hair and her clothes; it ran in at the top of her shoes and out at the heel, but she said that she was a real princess."
>
> —*The Princess and The Pea*, Hans Christian Andersen

The Real Princess

The tale of *The Princess and the Pea* was originally written by Hans Christian Andersen and first published in 1835. The drama unfolds as the search for a real princess begins. How does one know a real princess? If not by her clothes, then by a very small pea. The story leaves us to imagine the beautiful wardrobe that will grace the princess after she marries the prince. Of course, in storybook style and in every girl's dream, she has lovely gowns with silk

Riley, 7½ inches, by Kish & Company, wears a Classic Princess costume with V-ed inset and peplum.

their Distinctive Styles

Leeann, 11 inches, by Affordable Designs, wears a Classic Princess costume with gathered cap sleeve.

ribbons and peplums and lacy slips and sparkle.

The gathered cap sleeve SL1 is used for the Classic Princess designs. This sleeve pattern is perfect for sheer fabrics.

An easy Classic version (see photo above right) shows the scoop neckline with the shortened waistline, pattern piece B1(BF1 and BB1 for a 12-inch doll), and the gathered skirt S1. The sleeves and outer skirt are made from a sheer, dotted shimmery organza. The bodice and underskirt are satin. The hair accessories are made from purchased craft flowers and satin ribbons. White trim is applied to the waist and hem.

For a more detailed Classic design, use the same pattern pieces, but include the V-ed inset B4 and the peplum P (see Riley as the Real Princess, opposite page). The bodice is cut at the normal waistline and the V-ed inset is stitched in place before the sleeves are attached. The peplum is stitched to the bodice after the side seams are stitched and before the skirt is attached. See the General Instructions (Chapter 8) for details.

The Old World design is similar, and uses the same bodice and peplum patterns. The skirt is made from pattern piece S2 (six to eight panels), and the gathered bodice inset B5 adds softness to the gown. Both the peplum and the bodice inset can be cut from chiffon or organza. Pattern piece SL5 can be used to make a waist sash; shown is a complementary silk satin ribbon. A glimmer of pink from the pink tulle slip shines through the cream-colored skirt. Silk ribbon roses and satin bows decorate the gown in Real Princess style.

Little Darling, 13 inches, by The Doll Studio, is costumed in Old World Princess style.

Alice, Drink Me, illustration by John Tenniel, 1865

"If I had a world of my own, everything would be nonsense. Nothing would be what it is, because everything would be what it isn't. And contrary wise, what is, it wouldn't be. And what it wouldn't be, it would. You see?"

—Alice, *The Adventures of Alice in Wonderland*, Lewis Carroll

Alice in Wonderland

In the curious narrative by Lewis Carroll, Alice wanders in a land of eccentric characters and aristocratic dilemma. Her circa-1865 Victorian dress has a full gathered skirt, puff sleeves and a white apron. While the original illustrations by John Tenniel were printed in black and white, *The Nursery "Alice,"* which is a shortened, *"from nought to five"* version, printed Tenniel's illustrations colored and enlarged. An 1890 illustration by Peter Newell shows Alice wearing the most recognizable, or perhaps most popular, adaptation, a classic blue dress and white apron. Illustrations rendered later by various artists show her dress or apron trimmed in red.

There are three apron styles to choose from; they include two skirt patterns and two bib patterns: A1, A2, A3, and A4. The apron length can be adjusted to your personal preference. Use pattern piece A5 for the apron ties, sizes 11 and 12. Ribbon ties are recommended for smaller dolls.

This Classic Alice rendition uses pattern pieces A1, A4 and A5 and is stitched in a cotton batiste and lace. For a neat finish, stitch the apron hem first, and then apply the trim over the hem stitching.

The Old World version is rendered in a

The modified apron worn by Bridget, 11 inches, molds by Expressions, as the Old World Alice is double-layered and self-lined, to match the visual sheerness of the bib.

crisp cotton organdy, using pattern pieces A2 and A4, with ribbon ties. The straps are made from the trim. The apron skirt is double layered and self lined, to match the visual sheerness of the bib. An insertion trim and silk ribbon roses are used to decorate the outer edges. To self line the apron skirt, cut two apron skirts, stitch the side and lower edges of the apron, right sides facing. Turn the apron skirt right side out and press before attaching the skirt to the apron bib and adding the trims.

Pattern pieces A1 and A3 are used for the Avant Garde apron. Wide lace decorates the bib and skirt and is stitched on before the skirt is gathered and attached to the bib. French lace and ribbon finish the outer edges; they are stitched on after the skirt is attached to the bib. A silk ribbon is used for the ties.

Classic Alice, 12 inches, by Dianna Effner Porcelain Dolls, with a Sweet Petite Body, by Expressions, wears an apron of cotton batiste and lace.

Little Bo Peep, illustration by Scott Gustafson. ©1990. All rights reserved. From Favorite Nursery Rhymes from Mother Goose, The Greenwich Workshop Press, 2007. Used with permission.

"Little Bo Peep has lost her sheep
And can't tell where to find them.
Leave them alone, and they'll come
  home,
Wagging their tails behind them."

—Author Unknown

Little Bo Peep

Who does not remember this favorite nursery rhyme from their childhood? While the poem *Little Bo Peep* is perhaps pre-Victorian, Scott Gustafson's popular contemporary illustration brings to life this delightful poetic quandary. Faced with the worry over her lost sheep, Little Bo Peep is ever adorable in ruffled pantaloons, slips and a bonnet.

The hat is made from two pattern pieces (H2 and H4) and ribbon ties. Select different fabrics and trims to achieve the various silhouettes.

The Classic version is stitched in a cotton print; the narrow picot trim is stitched on before the ruffle is attached to the back of the bonnet. The Old World hat is made of a very soft silk charmeuse; to add volume, the hat portion is interfaced with the organza that is used on the hat ruffle, peplum and waist sash. The lace on the ruffle is stitched near the ruffle's fold and not on the gathered seam that connects the ruffle to the hat. The Twenty-First-Century Avant Garde Little Bo Peep uses the same hat and ruffle pattern. The hat is made from iridescent silk Doupioni that is dotted with French knots; the hat ruffle is cut on the bias and the fold is not pressed.

Classic Little Bo Peep, modeled by Allison, 11 inches, molds by Expressions, wears a bonnet with picot trim.

Old World Little Bo Peep, 10 inches, modeled by Tuesday's Child, 10 inches, by Boneka, wears a silk charmeuse and organza bonnet with French lace.

Bridget, 12 inches, molds by Expressions, wears an Avant Garde Little Bo Peep bonnet of silk Doupioni with embroidered French knots.

Riley, 7½ inches, by Kish & Company is costumed as a Classic Little Bo Peep.

Original costume sketch for The Nutcracker, by Ivan Vzevolozhsky, 1892

"The Nutcracker clapped his hands, and several little shepherds and shepherdesses, hunters and huntresses appeared, all so white you'd have thought they were made of pure sugar. ...Now they brought up a dear little golden chair, put in a white licorice cushion, and ever so graciously bade Marie be seated. She had no sooner done so than the shepherds and shepherdesses danced a charming ballet..."

—*The Nutcracker and the Mouse King,* E.T.A. Hoffmann

Sugar Plum Fairy

Sometimes storybooks become ballets, as did the Christmas tale of *The Nutcracker and the Mouse King,* by E.T.A. Hoffmann. *The Nutcracker* was first performed in 1982, at the Mariinsky Theatre, in St. Petersburg, Russia, to music composed by Pyotr Tchaikovsky. It is a romantic story of dolls and dancing, in a Land of Sweets where the Sugar Plum Fairy takes center stage.

The skirts on the Sugar Plum Fairy costumes are cut from tulle, illusion or sparkle illusion. These fabrics vary in width, from 45 inches to 108 inches. Layer several colors together to create depth and interest. Refer to the General Instructions (Chapter 8) for easy sewing and cutting directions.

The 11-inch Classic Sugar Plum Fairy skirt includes eight layers, sandwiching four layers of butterscotch sparkle illusion between four layers of pink tulle. The

The Classic Sugar Plum Fairy skirt for an 11-inch doll, modeled by Bridget, molds by Expressions, has eight layers of pink tulle and butterscotch sparkle illusion.

The Classic Sugar Plum Fairy's tutu for an 8-inch doll layers cream sparkle illusion with pink tulle. It is worn by Riley, 7½ inches, by Kish & Company.

On the Old World Sugar Plum Fairy costume worn by Tuesday's Child, 10 inches, by Boneka, the tulle is trimmed with beaded lace.

8-inch Classic Sugar Plum Fairy uses four layers of cream sparkle illusion over four layers of bright pink tulle. The skirts may be cut short or long and are stitched to the dropped-waist bodice B3 (BF3 and BB3 for a 12-inch doll). The same treatment is used on the sleeves, using pattern piece S5. The 11-inch Classic Sugar Plum Fairy is shown with eight layers of tulle on the sleeve, and the 8-inch Classic Sugar Plum Fairy is shown with two layers of tulle on the sleeves.

The Old World Sugar Plum Fairy shows four layers of bright-pink sparkle illusion sandwiched between four layers of cream tulle. Beaded lace is hand-stitched to the top layer of tulle.

Snow White, illustration by Franz Jüttner, 1905

Snow White

Snow White is a beautiful young princess and, as the mirror on the wall proclaims, "the fairest of them all." As told by the Brothers Grimm in the European tale, the Queen, her jealous stepmother, plots to take her life. But Snow White escapes into the forest and is eventually saved by the prince. Dressed with appropriate sweet and youthful innocence, she often wears a costume featuring a fitted bodice and an apron.

Three bodice and sleeve applications are used to create these Snow White costume interpretations. The Classic version, designed for simple sewing, uses the scoop-neck bodice pattern B1 (BF1 and BB1 for a 12-inch doll), and the sleeve pattern SL1. For the empire bodice, cut the fabric at the "shorten or lengthen here" markings on the B1 pattern piece, front and back. Stitch the trims and lace to the folded sleeve fabric before gathering and attaching to the bodice. Repeat the trim and lace decorations on the A1 apron. This design uses the S2 skirt pattern.

The Bavarian-inspired Old World Snow White uses the square neckline pattern B2 (BF2 and BB2 for a 12-inch doll) and sleeve pattern SL4. The square neckline is

The Bavarian-style Old World Snow White costume, modeled by Little Lou, 11 inches, by Dianna Effner Porcelain Dolls, has ribbon-trimmed sleeves.

The Avant Garde Snow White costume for a 10-inch doll, worn by Tuesday's Child, by Boneka, features a low waistline and ribbon sleeves.

Leeann, 11 inches, by Affordable Designs, is costumed as Classic Snow White, with an empire-style scoop-necked bodice, and decorated cap sleeves.

used to accommodate the straight edge of the lace trim. The lace trim is stitched to the basic bodice front before attaching the sleeves so that the raw edges of the lace are encased in the seam allowance. Ribbon trims the sleeve and is stitched in place while the sleeve is flat, before gathering the lower edge for the cuff or stitching it to the bodice.

For a lower waistline in the Avant Garde rendition, use bodice pattern piece B3 (BF3 and BB3 for a 12-inch doll). The sleeve SL5 is cut from ribbon; the ribbon is also stitched on the lower edge of the pantaloons P3. The center-front ribbon trim is repeated on the shimmery organza skirt S3. There are four layers of tulle in the slip.

*Little Red Riding Hood,
illustration by Gustave
Doré, 1867*

*Little Red Riding Hood,
illustration by George
Frederic Watts, 1890*

"Once upon a time there lived in a certain village a little country girl, the prettiest creature that ever was seen."

—*Little Red Riding Hood*,
Charles Perrault

Little Red Riding Hood

"Beware of strangers, little one," is the sentiment of the perennially popular tale of *Little Red Riding Hood*. Charles Perrault penned his version in his collection of stories entitled *Tales of Mother Goose* in 1697; in 1812 Jacob and Wilhelm Grimm published their version as *Little Red Cap* in the first volume of their collected *Children and Household Tales*. Little Red Riding Hood is dressed for travel; she wears a red cape and hood as she ventures through the woods to visit her ailing grandmother.

There are two hood and two cape styles to choose from. If the fabric is light-weight, the capes and hood may be self-lined. For a heavier fabric, such as wool, a lightweight lining is recommended.

The Classic hood and cape are made using pattern pieces H1 and H3. Stitch the darts in the hood, cape and lining pieces. The pieces are stitched together and gathered to fit. The neckline seam is finished with the ribbon that is used for the ties. See the General Instructions (Chapter 8).

The Old World hood and cape are stitched in an iridescent silk taffeta, and the Little Bo Peep bonnet pattern is used for the hood and a straight-cut cape. Cutting directions for the cape are found in the Cutting Dimensions Guide in the Patterns section. The hood ruffle is cut on the bias. Use H2 and H4 for the hood.

The Classic Little Red Riding Hood cape and hood is worn by Tuesday's Child, 10 inches, by Boneka.

Little Darling, 13 inches, by The Doll Studio, wears the Avant Garde Little Red Riding Hood in black and red silk jacquard, trimmed with a diminutive black ruffle.

Bridget, 11 inches, re-sculpted by Dianna Effner, wears an Old World Little Red Riding Hood costume with hood and cape of iridescent silk taffeta.

The Avant Garde cape and hood are self-lined and stitched in a black and red silk jacquard. A purchased ruffled trim is sandwiched in the outer seam. Use hood pattern piece H1 and the straight-cut cape (see the Cutting Dimensions Guide in the Patterns section). The cape and hood are completed with black silk ribbon ties.

Heidi, illustration by Rudolf Münger, 1880

"She did not look more than five years old, if as much, but what her natural figure was like, it would have been hard to say, for she had apparently two, if not three dresses, one above the other, and over these a thick red woollen [sic] shawl wound round about her, so that the little body presented a shapeless appearance, as, with it small feet shod in thick, nailed mountain-shoes, . . ."

—*Heidi*, Johanna Spyri

Heidi

Heidi, written by Swiss author Johanna Spyri, has captured the hearts of young and old alike. The young girl, raised by her grandfather, engages those she meets on her journeys with tenacious affection. Her humble upbringing is reflected in her clothing, except for the garments she receives while staying with Clara. She wears simple dresses, aprons, some flowers, and sometimes a shawl to ward off the cool mountain air.

The vest V pattern may be adapted for different applications. For a detached vest, use faux suede or felt fabric. The Classic vest uses vest pattern V, with the center back placed on the fold. It is made from faux suede, which requires no lining or hemming. This is recommended for all detached vests. Machine- or hand-stitch the vest detail. The nosegay is secured with quick drying fabric glue; flowers are made from silk embroidery ribbon.

The Old World Heidi rendition has a lined vest that is attached to the bodice. The center front seam may be placed on the fold for an overlapping vest, or stitched, to narrow the vest. See General Instructions (Chapter 8) for details. Beads are used to create faux grommets; silk embroidery ribbon is laced between the stitches that secure the beads.

Classic Heidi's faux-suede vest boasts a ribbon rose nosegay.

Johanna Spyri

Heidi.

Mit vielen Bildern von Rudolf Münger.

*Heidi, illustration by
Rudolf Münger, 1880*

*The Old World Heidi costume, worn by Little Lou II,
11 inches, molds by Expressions, has an attached silk
Doupioni vest; sheer floral ribbon and insertion lace
trim the apron.*

*Tuesday's Child, 10 inches, by Boneka, wears the
Classic Heidi costume.*

Juliet, or The Blue Necklace, by John William Waterhouse, 1898

Layers of detail and color on the Old World Juliet are achieved with intricate trims, beads, lace and ribbons.

"For I ne're saw true beauty till this night."

—Romeo, *Romeo and Juliet*,
William Shakespeare

Juliet

Juliet Capulet and Romeo Montague are at the heart of Shakespeare's classic play of *Romeo and Juliet*. "Two households, both alike in dignity, in fair Verona,"[1] begins this story of doomed young love. And while the drama ends with a tragic misunderstanding, young Juliet's passion remains legendary. Dates surrounding the play suggest the costumes were circa 1580s. During this era, women wore gowns over chemises with "richness in material and decoration, hose and a laced corset."[2]

Juliet's costumes have layers of detail that can be easily achieved with the use of intricate trims, beads, lace and ribbons. Gathered lace is appliquéd to the shortened square-neck bodice B2 (BF2 and BB2 for a 12-inch doll); to avoid extra seam bulk, the bodice is made from a lightweight lining fabric. The vest pattern V is shortened and used for the bodice overdress, then trimmed with beads. A metallic picot braid is used for the cuff on the puff sleeve SL5 and for trimming the overskirt. Six panels of pattern piece S2 create the overskirt: they are layered over the gathered chiffon skirt S1. The chiffon skirt is lined with a lightweight lining fabric using the S1 pattern.

Silk embroidery ribbons cascade from the cap, repeating shades of colors used in the dress and ribbon roses. See the General Instructions (Chapter 8) for cap, sleeve and lace appliqué directions.

The Old World Juliet's wired cap is trimmed with ruffled lace, metallic trim and silk embroidery ribbon.

Bridget, 11 inches, by Dianna Effner Porcelain Dolls, is costumed as Old World Juliet.

"In theatre, a triple threat is (to) sing, dance, and act. If you walk on (stage) and there are more than three triple threats, and you are not a triple threat, walk out.

Every design needs the *triple threat* or a 1, 2, 3 punch: overall look, fit, details.

A Designer Triple Threat: Tenacity, Talent, Time (patience)"

—Christina Bougas, Creator of Clea Bella

1. William Shakespeare, Prologue, *Romeo and Juliet.*

2. Francois Boucher, *20,000 Years of Fashion* (New York, Harry N. Abrams, Inc. Publishers, 1966).

Chapter 2

Classic and Endearing Style

What is more classic than *Once upon a time*? It is when storybooks are read and listened to and imagined; it is where the storybook characters gain their endearing style. Certain costume elements, such as color or design, are indelibly associated with certain storybook characters. For instance, we most often think of Alice in Wonderland wearing a blue dress with a white apron or pinafore, and Little Red Riding Hood is always adorned with a red cape and hood or cap. The Classic patterns range in difficulty from easy to moderate, but some general sewing knowledge is necessary. Please refer to the General Instructions (Chapter 8) for the basic sewing assembly steps. Pattern pieces are presented for each design in each of the four sizes: 7½-to 8-inch doll; 10-inch doll; 11-inch doll and 12-inch doll.

"Once upon a time, a queen was doing needle work while staring outside her window at the beautiful snow."

—*Snow White and the Seven Dwarfs*, Jacob and Wilhelm Grimm

The Real Princess

To make this costume, use these pattern pieces.

B1 Bodice – Scoop Neckline
    (BF1 and BB1 for 12-inch doll)
SL1 Sleeve – Gathered Cap
S1 Skirt Gathered

To make this costume, use these pattern pieces.

B2 Bodice – Square Neckline
    (BF2 and BB2 for 12-inch doll)
B4 Bodice V-Shaped Inset
SL1 Sleeve – Gathered Cap
S1 Skirt and Slip – Gathered
P Peplum

Alice in Wonderland

To make this costume, use these pattern pieces.

B1 Bodice – Scoop Neckline
  (BF1 and BB1 for 12-inch doll)
SL3 Sleeve – Gathered Medium
S1 Skirt and Slip – Gathered
A1 Apron
A4 Apron – Bib
A5 Apron – Straps
P2 Pantaloons – Full

To make this costume, use these pattern pieces.

B1 Bodice – Scoop Neckline
  (BF1 and BB1 for 12-inch doll)
SL3 Sleeve – Gathered Medium
S1 Skirt and Slip – Gathered
C Collar
P2 Pantaloons – Full
A1 Apron
A4 Apron – Bib
A5 Apron – Straps (See Cutting Dimensions Guide in
  Pattern section for ties)
SK Socks

Little Bo Peep

To make this costume, use these pattern pieces.

B2 Bodice – Square Neckline (BF2 and BB2 for 12-inch doll)
SL2 Sleeve – Gathered Short
S1 Skirt and Slip – Gathered
P1 Pantaloons – Straight Leg, with lower ruffle (See General Instructions for ruffle details)
H2 Hat
H4 Hat Ruffle
C1 Corset

To make this costume, use these pattern pieces.

B2 Bodice (BF2 and BB2 for 12-inch doll)
SL3 Sleeve – Gathered Medium
S1 Skirt and Slip – Gathered
P1 Pantaloons – Straight Leg
H2 Hat or Hood
H4 Hat or Hood Ruffle
C1 Corset

Sugar Plum Fairy

To make this costume, use these pattern pieces.

B3 Bodice – Dropped Waist (BF3 and BB3 for 12-inch doll)
SL5 Sleeve – Puff Sleeve (Omit gathers on folded sleeve edge)
S1 Skirt – Gathered
BSL Ballet Slipper and SS Ballet Slipper Sole for 11- and 12-inch dolls
Purchased shoes for 7½- 8- and 10-inch dolls
Purchased tights

To make this costume, use these pattern pieces.

B3 Bodice – Dropped Waist (BF3 and BB3 for 12-inch doll)
SL5 Sleeve – Puff Sleeve (Omit gathers on folded sleeve edge)
S1 Skirt – Gathered, 8 layers
BSL Ballet Slipper
SS Ballet Slipper Sole

Snow White

To make this costume, use these pattern pieces.

B2 Bodice – Square Neckline (BF2 and BB2 for 12-inch doll)
B5 Bodice – Gathered Inset
SL3 Sleeve- Gathered Medium
S2 Skirt A-line Panel
A1 Apron
V Vest

To make this costume, use these pattern pieces.

B2 Bodice – Scoop Neckline (BF1 and BB1 for 12-inch doll) shortened
SL1 Sleeve – Gathered Cap
S2 Skirt – A-line Panel
A1 Apron
SK Sock

Little Red Riding Hood

To make this costume, use these pattern pieces.

B1 Bodice – Scooped Neckline (BF1 and BB1 for 12-inch doll)
SL4 Sleeve – Gathered Long
S1 Skirt and Slip Gathered
H1 Hood
H3 Cape

To make this costume, use these pattern pieces.

B1 Bodice – Scooped Neckline (BF1 and BB1 for 12-inch doll)
SL3 Sleeve – Gathered Medium
S2 Skirt – A-line Panel
A1 Apron
H1 Hood
H3 Cape
SK Sock

To make this costume, use these pattern pieces.

B1 Bodice – Scoop Neckline (BF1 and BB1 for 12-inch doll)
SL 2 Sleeve – Gathered Medium
S1 Skirt and Slip – Gathered
A1 Apron
V Vest
C Collar
SK Sock

To make this costume, use these pattern pieces.

B2 Bodice – Square Neckline (BF2 and BB2 for 12-inch doll)
SL4 Sleeve – Gathered Long
S2 Skirt – A-line Panel, 8 panels
Straight-cut gathered lace skirt inset (See Cutting
    Dimensions Guide in Patterns section)
JC Juliet/ Ballerina Cap
Ribbon trim bodice inset

"I consider my doll clothes more like miniature fashions and try to include as many details as possible in each one of them. When such a detail is discovered by the collector a whole new surge of excitement comes with it and this is what I aspire to. Dolls are there to make us dream and allow us to be excited again and again about the little details. I hope everyone finds time to include...their own excitement in the garments they will create...as I know there will be someone, somewhere to feel it and appreciate it when looking at the results."

—Denis Bastien,
Leeann's "Dad," Affordable Designs

Chapter 3

Old-World Elegance and Charm

Costumes with old-world elegance and charm are evocative of antique dolls with small samplings of delicate lace and luxurious fabrics artfully showcased on each garment. These renditions are designed to have a beautiful heirloom quality with contemporary appeal. The Old World patterns include a bit more detail than the Classic patterns, but most only require additional layers of straight stitching and are not considerably more difficult. While these designs are shown in silks and fine trims, they can be attractive in any fabric that is suitable for doll costuming. See Selecting Fabrics and Trims (Chapter 5). Study the pictures and develop your own design elegance and charm.

> "What's in a name? That which we call a rose
>
> By any other name would smell as sweet."
>
> —Juliet, *Romeo and Juliet*, William Shakespeare

The Real Princess

To make this costume, use these pattern pieces.

B2 Bodice – Square Neckline (BF2 and BB2 for 12-inch doll)
B5 Bodice – Gathered Inset
SL1 Sleeve – Gathered Cap
SL5 (Use sleeve pattern for waist sash, cut to fit on doll)
S2 Skirt – A-line Panel, 8 panels
P Peplum

To make this costume, use these pattern pieces.

B2 Bodice – Square Neckline, shortened (BF2 and BB2 for 12-inch doll)
B5 Bodice – Gathered Inset
SL2 Sleeve – Gathered Short
S2 Skirt – A-line Panel
P Peplum
Ribbon waist sash

Alice in Wonderland

To make this costume, use these pattern pieces.

B1 Bodice – Scoop Neckline (BF1 and BB1 for 12-inch doll)
SL3 Sleeve – Gathered Medium
S1 Skirt and Slip – Gathered
A3 Apron – Bib and Straps
A1 Apron

To make this costume, use these pattern pieces.

B1 Bodice (BF1 and BB1 for 12-inch doll)
SL2 Sleeve – Gathered Short
S1 Skirt and Slip – Gathered
P2 Pantaloons – Full
A4 Apron – Bib
A2 Apron – Modified Skirt

Little Bo Peep

Sugar Plum Fairy

To make this costume, use these pattern pieces.

B1 Bodice – Scooped Neckline (BF1 and BB1 for 12-inch doll)
SL2 Sleeve – Gathered Short
S1 Skirt and Slip – Gathered
P1 Pantaloons – Straight Leg
H2 Hat
H4 Hat Ruffle
P Peplum
SL5 (Use sleeve pattern for waist sash, cut to fit on doll)

To make this costume, use these pattern pieces.

B1 Bodice – Scoop Neckline (BF1 and BB1 for 12-inch doll)
SL5 Sleeve – Puff Sheer
S1 Skirt – Gathered
PH Princess Hat

Snow White

Little Red Riding Hood

To make this costume, use these pattern pieces.

B2 Bodice – Square Neckline (BF2 and BB2 for 12-inch doll)
SL4 Sleeve – Gathered Long
S1 Skirt and Slip – Gathered
A1 Apron
Straight-cut Cape (See Cutting Dimensions Guide in Patterns section) Gather to fit neckline and finish with a bias cut casing.

To make this costume, use these pattern pieces.

B2 Bodice – Square Neckline (BF2 and BB2 for 12-inch doll)
B5 Bodice – Gathered Inset
SL 4 Sleeve – Gathered Long
S1 Skirt and Slip – Gathered
H2 Hood
H4 Hood Ruffle
Straight-cut Cape (See Cutting Dimensions Guide in Patterns section)
C1 Corset

Heidi

To make this costume, use these pattern pieces.

B1 Bodice – Scoop Neckline (BF1 and BB1 for 12-inch doll)
SL3 Sleeve – Medium Gathered
S1 Skirt and Slip – Gathered
P2 Pantaloons – Full
A1 Apron
V Vest
S Scarf
SK Socks

Juliet

To make this costume, use these pattern pieces.

B2 Bodice – Square Neckline, shortened (BF2 and BB2 for 12-inch doll)
V Vest, shortened
SL5 Sleeve – Puff Sheer
S1 Skirt and Slip – Gathered, for under skirt
S2 Skirt A-line Panel – for over skirt
JC Juliet Ballerina Cap

"When I make a doll, the most important thing to me is the expression. The doll seems to be speaking to me, telling her story. The costume should serve to develop the story with its shapes, colors and details. The costume should supplement and reflect the facial expression. Then a satisfying unity is achieved. The ideal art doll, I think, is a doll that radiates expression in every detail."

—Dianna Effner, Dianna Effner Porcelain Dolls

Chapter 4

Twenty-First-Century Avant Garde

Add the element of imagination to your costumes for an avant-garde flair. Liberties are taken with the classic storybook style and silhouette to create the Twenty-First-Century Avant Garde patterns. Tulle slips, interesting trims and delightful color combinations add whimsy to each design, as do the diverse hemlines and lengths. Allow yourself the freedom to experiment a little and include an unexpected design surprise. If the doll begins to dance in your hands, you have discovered the joy of costume design.

"Alice thought she had never seen such a curious croquet ground in her life: it was all ridges and furrows; the croquet balls were live hedgehogs, and the mallets live flamingoes, and the soldiers had to double themselves up and stand on their hands and feet, to make the arches."

—*Alice's Adventures in Wonderland*, Lewis Carroll

Alice Managing her Flamingo,
illustration by John Tenniel, 1865

The Real Princess

Alice in Wonderland

To make this costume, use these pattern pieces.

B2 Bodice – Square Neckline (BF2 and BB2 for 12-inch doll)
SL3 Sleeve – Gathered Medium
S2 Skirt – A-line Panel and Tear Drop
S1 Skirt and Slip – Gathered (See General Instructions – Exposed Under Skirt)
Ruffle (See Cutting Dimensions Guide in Patterns section)
P Peplum
SL5 (Use sleeve pattern for waist sash, cut to fit on doll)
PH Princess Hat (Add bias cut sash to hat edge)

To make this costume, use these pattern pieces.

B1 Bodice (BF1 and BB1 for 12-inch doll)
SL2 Sleeve – Gathered Short
S3 Skirt – A-line Modified Panel
S1 Slip – Gathered
P1 Pantaloons – Straight Leg
A3 Apron – Bib and Straps
A1 Apron
SK socks

Little Bo Peep

To make this costume, use these pattern pieces.

B2 Bodice – Square Neckline (BF2 and BB2 for 12-inch doll)
B4 Bodice – V-Shaped Inset
SL5 Sleeve – Sheer Puff
S1 Skirt & Slip – Gathered
P3 Pantaloons – Very Full
H2 Hat or Hood
H4 Hat or Hood Ruffle
SK Sock

To make this costume, use these pattern pieces.

B2 Bodice – Square Neckline (BF2 and BB2 for 12-inch doll)
SL 2 Sleeve – Gathered Short
S1 Skirt and Slip – Gathered (skirt: 2 layers; slip: 4 layers)
P3 Pantaloons – Very Full
H2 Hat or Hood
H4 Hat or Hood Ruffle, includes tulle ruffle

Sugar Plum Fairy

Snow White

To make this **advanced** costume, use these pattern pieces.

B2 Bodice – Square Neckline (BF2 and BB2 for 12-inch doll)
B4 Bodice – V-Shaped Inset
S5 Sleeve –Gathered Puff
S1 Skirt and Slip – Gathered (Add fabric or lace ruffle to skirt, cut twice the fullness of the skirt)
P3 Pantaloons – Very Full
PH Princess Hat
SK Sock

To make this costume, use these pattern pieces.

B3 Bodice – Dropped Waist (BF3 and BB3 for 12-inch doll)
SL5 Sleeve – Sheer Puff, use ribbon width
S3 Skirt – A-line Modified Panel, 8 panels
S1 Skirt and Slip – Gathered, 4 layers tulle
P3 Pantaloons – Very Full
SK Socks

Little Red Riding Hood

Heidi

To make this **advanced** costume, use these pattern pieces.

B3 Bodice – Dropped Waist (BF3 and BB3 for 12-inch doll)
SL5 Sleeve – Gathered Puff (Hand tack small pleats on
   sleeve edge or gathered effect)
S3 Skirt – A-line Modified Panel, 8 panels
S1 Skirt and Slip – Gathered, 4 layers tulle
P3 Pantaloons – Very Full with long cuff
H1 Hood
Square-cut Cape (See Cutting Dimensions Guide in
   Patterns section)

To make this costume, use these pattern pieces.

B2 Bodice – Square Neckline (BF2 and BB2 for 12-inch doll)
SL4 Sleeve – Gathered Long
S1 Skirt and Slip – Gathered; 2 layers net
P3 Pantaloons – Very Full
A1 Apron
S Scarf

Juliet

To make this **easy** costume, use these pattern pieces.

B2 Bodice – Square Neckline (BF2 and BB2 for 12-inch doll)
SL2 Sleeve – Gathered Short
S2 Skirt – A-line and Tear Drop Panel
JC Juliet/Ballerina Cap

"...go beyond your imagination because there is no limit...because costume design is never done...because the more you do it the more creative you become."

—Ankie Daanen

Chapter 5 — Selecting Fabrics and Trims

Silk taffeta shimmers in the light and offers an adorable skirt silhouette; it is rounded out with layers of tulle slip. The dotted Swiss apron is trimmed in a very narrow woven braid and tied with a silk satin ribbon. Delicate French cotton lace decorates the apron and sleeve.

"And so it was indeed: she was now only ten inches high, and her face brightened up at the thought that she was now the right size for going through the little door into that lovely garden."

—*Alice's Adventures in Wonderland*, Lewis Carroll

Scale is everything in doll costuming, especially for small dolls. If only we could pour something from Alice's little bottle to make fabrics and trims shrink to size. Instead, the fun and challenge is to find suitable material and trimmings.

When choosing fabric, determine how the bulk from gathering and the folds for hems will affect the overall appearance and fit. Fold several fabric layers together to realize the volume or thickness that will result, and then imagine that stitched into the seam on a very small waistline.

It is often hard to know by just looking; a little fabric crunching works best. Consider the drape and hand of each fabric in relationship to the doll size and the desired silhouette of the costume. Some fabrics are woven with very fine threads but have a great deal of body and/or stiffness, while others are very soft and supple. The fabric you choose will affect the finished silhouette.

Natural fibers, such as silk and cotton, have more resilience than most synthetics and can more easily adapt to the small curves on collars and sleeves. The silk filaments used to weave material are very fine and generate a minimum amount of bulk in seams; this makes silk an excellent fabric choice for clothing small dolls. Common silk fabrics are taffeta and Doupioni; taffeta has a tighter weave and is generally easier to work with because it doesn't fray as easily. There are also many beautiful cotton fabrics to choose from, which are available in varying weights. Batiste and organdy

Little Bo Peep's skirt, bodice, hat and pantaloons are made of silk charmeuse, which contrasts in color and texture with the peplum, waist sash and hat ruffle made from sheer shimmery organza.

Choose small prints to keep the costume in scale. Consider the size of the doll's hand in comparison to the motif. A lightweight wool with an acetate lining works well with the polyester ribbon ties. The soft melon color of the ribbon coordinates with the dress print and is not overwhelming next to her face.

Silk jacquard is used for both costumes. A narrow check ribbon on Riley's dress replicates the woven braid used on Little Darling's dress. The black ruffle trim on the larger hood and cape is omitted from the smaller costume because it would be too stiff. Silk embroidery ribbon is used for the small costume ties; ¼-inch silk satin ribbon is used on the larger costume.

have very fine weaves and are ideal for little aprons, collars and cuffs.

Consider the overall scale when selecting prints. Tiny flowers spaced far apart

may allow for only one or two flowers on a bodice or sleeve. The same is true for plaids; what seems like a small plaid may look like large square blocks on an 8-inch doll. Think small, and then think smaller.

Laces and trims require similar consideration. Choose lace, trims and ribbons that are soft and supple. Of course, scale is important, but trims present an additional bulk factor and are often too stiff for small dolls. Some trims and ribbons are not colorfast or washable, which is important to consider if the doll clothes are being made for children to play with. Heirloom-quality French lace has a very fine weave and its beautiful, intricate detail adds charm and distinction to doll costumes. Silk embroidery ribbon is perfect for ribbon roses or ties on corsets and bonnets.

Fine fabric stores, craft and scrap-booking shops and online doll crafting/costuming sites are good resources but consider, too, acquiring remnant pieces of lace or fabrics from alteration shops and bridal salons. There are some great storybook treasures on their sewing-room floors.

Combine elements of softness, pattern and structure. Here, the soft drape of the sleeve, the body of the peplum and slip and the pattern of the lace add interest and appeal.

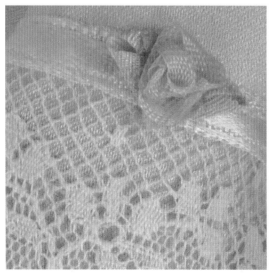

Ribbon roses made from silk embroidery ribbon add accent colors to the aqua, ivory and soft-blue palette.

Chapter 6

Sewing for Small Dolls

> "Sometimes we start with interesting fabric; sometimes we have an idea and make sketches, and then look for fabric. I like to pin it all on the doll and try different things . . . and after a few days I think of changes. Sometimes, if I don't like it, I put it in the garbage."
>
> —Zofia Zawieruszynski, Zawieruszynski Originals

Little doll clothes require small pattern pieces, and small pattern pieces require their own unique set of skills, from cutting to sewing to finishing. Collect a few basic sewing supplies and use the following tips for optimum results.

Tracing and Cutting Pattern Pieces

To begin, trace the pattern pieces with a pencil, rather than a pen, to avoid transferring ink smudges onto the fabric. Cut the pattern pieces out before placing them on the fabric and duplicate the pattern markings; use a clear ruler to draw straight edges and straight-of-grainlines.

Cutting Tips

Use a rotary cutter and clear ruler to cut all straight edges. First, pin each pattern piece to the fabric following the straight-of-grainline guide. To avoid cutting into the seam allowance, place a clear ruler on top of the pattern piece and fabric along the straight edges. Use gentle pressure on the ruler as you cut to help stabilize the fabric beneath it.

Pin curved pattern pieces, like the bodice or sleeve, to the fabric. Cut these pinned sections away from the rest of the fabric while leaving at least one inch of fabric on all sides. Use a clear ruler and rotary cutter to cut the straight edges,

Recommended Sewing Supplies

Rotary cutter and cutting board

Clear ruler

Dressmaker and embroidery scissors

Sewing machine needles:
  sizes 10/70, 11/75

Sharps hand needles
  (I recommend 10 sharps)

Thread of good quality

5mm snaps

Silk pins

Tear-away stabilizer

Fray block product

Measuring tape

Quick-set fabric glue

Long doll needle or stiletto

Small crochet hook
  (I recommend size 5)

A fine paint brush or eyeliner brush

such as the side, shoulder or underarm edges. Use sharp scissors to cut the remaining curved edges.

To keep small or loosely woven pieces from fraying, use a fine paint brush to apply a fray block product to the cutting edge. The fray block may seep slightly, especially on silks, so be careful to keep it

within the ¼-inch seam allowance. Allow the fray block to dry and then cut the pattern pieces, as suggested above. Note: The fray block may also be applied after the fabric pieces are cut.

Use a fray block product on the cut ribbon ends, as well. For a crisp, straight cut, use a rotary cutter to re-trim the ribbon edges after the fray block has dried. To properly gauge the desired length on streamers and ties, trim the ribbons after the costume is finished and the doll is dressed.

Tear-away stabilizer supports the fabric while stitching. It is especially helpful to use when stitching together small or lightweight fabric pieces, or when applying piping or lace trims. Several varieties are available; it can be purchased by the roll or by the yard. Keep small torn-away stabilizer remnants to reuse on short seams. Quilting and sewing machine shops, as well as general fabric stores, often stock these products.

Stitching Tips

Use a small-sized sewing machine needle, such as a 10 or 11, and thread of good quality. Threads with a finer twist add less bulk to tiny seam allowances; they are also less likely to jam the sewing machine on short seams.

When stitching short seams, layer the fabric pieces over a piece of tear-away stabilizer. Start the stitching on the stabilizer, take several stitches onto the fabric before backstitching, and then complete the seam. When the stitching is complete, gently tear away the stabilizer.

Try this method when stitching together small lined pieces, such as a collar. First, cut out the top layer and place it, right sides facing, on the uncut lining and tear-away stabilizer. Be sure to keep the grainlines straight. Stitch the pieces together, trim the excess fabric along the cutting line, and then gently tear away the stabilizer. It is easier to trim the fabric with the stabilizer in place.

Gathering Tips

Stitch two rows of gathering stitches on all gathered seams. The double rows will keep the seam allowance flat and expose a clear seam line. Use a doll needle or stiletto to adjust the gathers while stitching, and to gently expose the tiny pleats that are formed by the pulled threads. This makes the stitching process easier and yields excellent results. Be careful to keep the stiletto point clear of the sewing machine needle while you are stitching. It is often helpful to use tear-away stabilizer for these seams, as well.

For easy stitching, layer small fabric pieces on tear-away stabilizer.

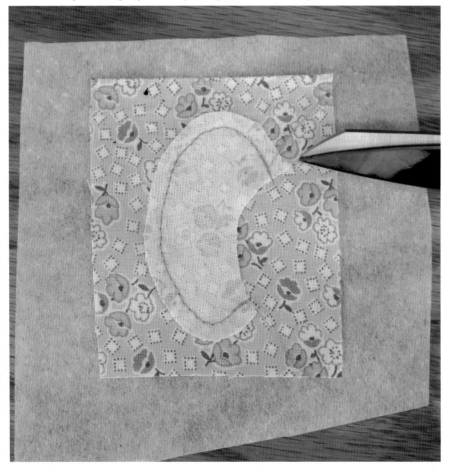

Thread Tips

When stitching ribbon trim to fabric, use matching machine embroidery thread for the top thread. This thread is finer and if you loosen the top thread tension slightly, the stitches almost disappear.

Turning Aid

Turn small bodices and sleeves right side out with a small crochet hook. Use the hook to start the fabric turning and then use the round end of the hook to push the fabric through the opening. Avoid using pins or needles to turn the fabric. The fabric threads from the narrow ¼-inch seam allowance may pull through, creating a messy seam finish.

Finishing Tips

While finishing the seam with a machine overlock stitch or serger is not necessary, it gives a more professional look to the finished costume. On small costumes, however, the process is often difficult because the little pieces seem to get lost under the presser foot. Therefore, limited serging is recommended for these costumes. Serge the center back edges of the skirts and slips before stitching the pieces together. Serge the bodice side seams after they are stitched together (optional) and serge the waistline. Trim all other seams neatly, between each step.

Use small snaps and closures; 5mm snaps are recommended. These are often referred to as doll closures and may be purchased in retail stores or through online sites.

Use quick-drying fabric glue to construct and attach ribbon roses. For better control, apply the glue with the tip of a doll needle or stiletto.

"I adore making doll clothes..."

—Martha Pullen, Publisher,
Sew Beautiful

Use a stiletto or doll needle (shown) to arrange gathers on a narrow seam allowance.

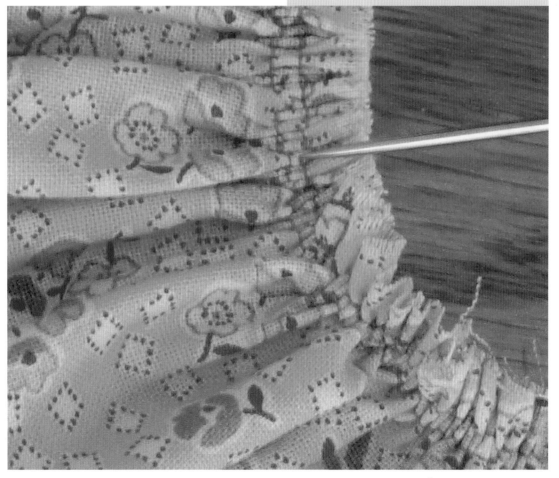

Chapter 7

Layers and Layers of Design Surprise

"... then she took twenty mattresses and laid them on the pea, and then she laid twenty eider-down beds on top of the mattress."

—*The Princess and the Pea,*
Hans Christian Andersen

Who can resist peeking under the layers of skirts on a beautiful doll to view the petticoats, and then lifting the petticoats for a peek at the pantaloons, only to be delighted by the ribbons that cascade from the mid-calf ties? Design surprise is whimsical, frivolous, enchanting and takes only a little imagination. Include a design surprise on every layer of your costume.

Design Surprise Details

Small horizontal pleats stitched onto the skirt add an easy-to-accomplish design element. The pleats add volume to the silhouette and are an excellent way to add structure to lightweight slip fabrics. Vary

Horizontal pleats, stitched on silk Doupioni, add volume to Old World Alice's skirt. Fabric variations include a cotton organdy apron, silk taffeta pantaloons and patterned stockings.

Insertion lace is used in a non-traditional fashion, bordering the apron's skirt and bib.

A single layer of point d'esprit (patterned net), trimmed with lace and ribbon roses, peaks beneath the skirt and rests on layers of tulle.

the pleat width or depth depending on the costume size and skirt length. Experiment on a scrap piece of fabric and hold it up the doll to determine the desired effect. Note: Horizontal pleats are not suitable for A-line panels.

Lace is a delightful detail on any costume. Stitch lace to the hemlines of skirts and slips. Use flat lace as you would a piece of fabric for pantaloon cuffs or layered on a bodice or apron. The color of the lace can be used to intensify or soften the color pallet. The contrast of white lace brightens colors, while an ivory, cream or off-white lace creates an old-world antique effect. When combining a variety of laces, choose laces that have common elements of color, texture or weight.

Add small color accents with ribbon roses or other floral decorations. Silk embroidery ribbon is very fine and lightweight, which makes it perfect for making beautiful diminutive roses. It can be purchased at craft or fabric stores in small two- or three-yard packages, or in specialty departments, by the yard. Excellent online directions for ribbon roses can be found by typing in the keyword "ribbon roses." Pre-made ribbon roses are also available at craft and fabric stores.

Tulle, net and illusion accents are an inexpensive way to add a design layer for slips, sleeves or ruffles. While commonly

Avant Garde Little Bo Peep's cotton print is in scale with the doll and the colors are accented by the trim, ribbons and tulle.

Double layers of folded tulle define Little Bo Peep's hat ruffle.

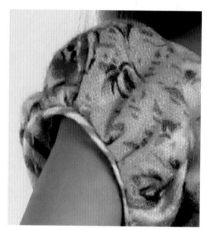

A bias-cut striped cuff adds interest to the short sleeve.

Alice's pantaloons are cuffed with the same 2-inch-wide lace that trims the point d'esprit slip.

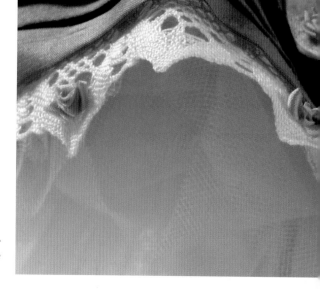

Four layers of tulle support the silhouette of Alice's skirt.

Layers and Layers of Design Surprise • 51

known for their use as wedding veils, these lightweight nets come in a variety of colors, variations and widths. Combine sparkle or glittered tulle for a festive appeal. Layer colors of tulle for visual depth and to achieve an iridescent appearance. Silk or cotton netting or tulle is often used for elegant costuming or consider point d'esprit—patterned netting that is available in a wide range of quality and price.

Braids and trims are also an excellent way to add whimsy to costumes. Consider including them in unexpected ways, such as horizontally stitched on the pantaloons or combining coordinating trims. Hand-stitch beaded wedding lace to tulle skirts or on a princess hat for an heirloom distinction. Often fabric outlets carry overstock trims from apparel manufac-

Alternating layers of pink tulle and butterscotch sparkle illusion create the iridescent appearance of the Classic Sugar Plum Fairy's tutu.

The Classic Sugar Plum Fairy's ballet slippers mirror the ribbon, rose and lace elements that decorate the bodice and hair accessories.

The sleeve and skirt colors are repeated in the hair accessory and on the ribbbon roses. Metallic lace juxtaposes the white lace and airy look of the sparkle illusion.

turers—trims that are not generally available at retail fabric shops but are also great finds for doll costuming.

Finally, perhaps the most important and easiest design surprise element for storybook dolls is ribbon. Include it as cascading streamers on hats or hair accessories or as tiny bows on slips or as a simply stitched trim on skirts; ribbon always adds design surprise and storybook charm.

"I have always felt that even the smallest detail on an outfit should be well thought out and executed. It is the small details that stand out and give quality to your conception, if well done. The combination, of colors and texture in particular, is always my starting point when designing my costumes. I start with the basic colors I want to use and then add one or two more of the complementary colors, which will be used for small details. This makes the detail and the costume come together."

—Maggie Iacono,
Maggie Made Dolls

A delicate red-and-black patterned jacquard is used for the hood and cape. Purchased ruffled frill gives form to the soft silhouette.

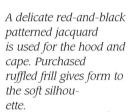

The Modified A-line Skirt pattern is used for Avant Garde appeal on Little Red Riding Hood's costume. The dress is stitched in a rich silk jacquard with silk organdy sleeves; it is layered over shimmery tulle and full silk taffeta pantaloons.

Complementary cream and black trims frame the skirt, bodice and pantaloons.

Layers of complementary colors—pinks and creams—are used for depth and texture on the Avant Garde Sugar Plum Fairy's costume. Beaded lace decorates the hat, bodice and tulle skirt.

Chapter 8

General Instructions

> "Read the directions and directly you will be directed in the right direction."
>
> -*Alice's Adventures in Wonderland*, Lewis Carroll

This chapter presents the general sewing instructions for costume assembly. It includes directions for the various bodice, skirt, sleeve and pantaloon patterns, and the additional accessories for each costume, including pattern alterations. The instructions refer to individual pattern pieces, not completed costumes. For instance: pattern piece B1 is for a basic bodice with a scoop neckline. Instructions are found for it under Bodice Variations; depending on the design you choose, everything relating to the bodice is found in this category. SL1 is the pattern piece for a cap sleeve; instructions for it and all other sleeves are found under Sleeve Variations. It may be helpful to choose the design that interests you and to study the instructions for each pattern piece listed for that costume before you begin.

Bodice Variations

Choose a pattern size that is closest to your doll's size. Make a sample lined bodice from a scrap piece of cotton fabric, without the sleeves, but including the side seams. Make necessary adjustments to the pattern before cutting the costume fabric. The sample should fit nicely around the neck and armholes, although not too tightly, and overlap at least ¼-inch at the back edge. The waist should be loose enough to allow ample room for the skirt's seam allowance. See Instructions for Adjusting Patterns on page 68, if necessary. Use a ¼-inch seam allowance for all seams, unless otherwise instructed.

Basic Bodice (Easy)

The bodice patterns are designed to be completely lined. For 7½- to 8-inch, 10-inch and 11-inch patterns (B1, B2 and B3), the front and back are combined into one piece. This eliminates the need for a shoulder seam and the extra bulk it creates at the neckline. For the basic bodice,

From left: Basic bodice stitching: turn the bodice right-side-out and press.

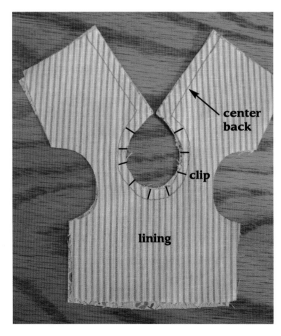

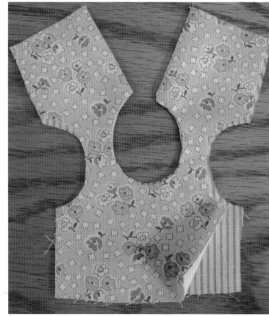

place the lining fabric on the bodice fabric, with right sides facing; stitch the back seam around the neck opening and down the other back edge. Clip the neckline curve and corners (for square neckline) and turn the bodice right side out; press the seamed edge. Baste the armhole and the lower edges of the bodice to the lining. For designs with collars, pin or baste the collar to the bodice before attaching the lining.

For a 12-inch doll, the bodice back pattern piece (BB1, BB2 or BB3) is used for the face fabric and the lining; the back edge is on the fold. With right sides facing, stitch the bodice-front fabric to the bodice back at the shoulder seams. Repeat for the bodice-front lining fabric. Complete the bodice as instructed above.

Square Neckline Bodice with V-ed Inset (Easy)

Use pattern pieces B2 (BF2 and BB2 for a 12-inch doll) and B4. Construct the basic bodice (see above). To prepare the V-ed inset, apply a fray block product to the raw edges; for lightweight fabrics, back the V-ed inset with an iron-on interfacing. Fold under the V-ed inset facing and press. Apply lace or trim to cover the raw edges. Position the decorated V-ed inset on top of the basic bodice and tack it at the armhole edges.

Attach the desired sleeves and skirts. Be careful not to stitch the lower V into the waistline seam.

Square Neckline with Lace or Ribbon Inset

Use pattern pieces B2 (BF2 and BB2 for a 12-inch doll). Construct the basic bodice (see above). For a detailed bodice front, layer lace or ribbon trim across the square neckline of the bodice. Layer the trim above the waist seam-line to maintain the trim's scalloped or decorative edge. Baste the trim to the side and to the

The 12-inch bodice has shoulder seams.

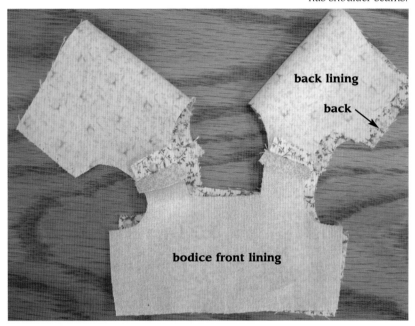

back lining

back

bodice front lining

Far left: pin collars to the bodice before attaching the lining.

Left: tack the v-ed inset at the armhole edges.

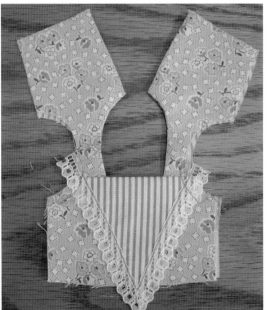

Use lace or ribbon to decorate the square neckline bodice.

armhole edges and across the neckline edge before attaching the sleeves.

Square Neckline Bodice with Gathered Inset (Intermediate)

Use pattern pieces B2 (BF2 and BB2 for a 12-inch doll) and B5. Construct the basic bodice (see pages 54-55). Run a gathering stitch across the top, middle (optional) and bottom of the gathered inset B5. Evenly draw all three rows of gathering stitches until the inset fits on the bodice front at the armhole and side edges. Place the bodice-front neckline across the top row of gathering stitches on the inset, with right sides facing. To secure the inset, stitch across the entire bodice front at the neckline edge. Fold the inset down to cover the bodice front. Stitch the lower gathered edge of the inset to the bodice-front waistline. Stitch along the center row of gathering stitches to secure the inset to the bodice front (optional). Note: The desired fullness of the inset may vary depending on the style and the weight of the inset fabric. Trim the width, if necessary.

Stitch the inset at the neckline edge.

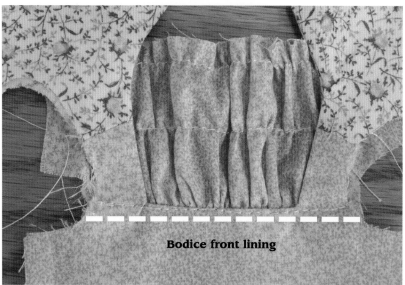

Bodice front lining

Fold the inset to cover the bodice front, as indicated by the curved arrow.

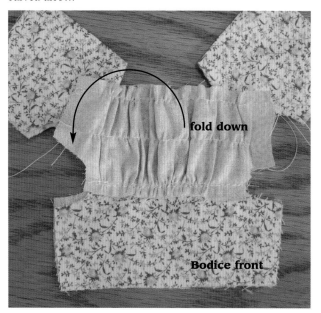

fold down

Bodice front

Stitch the inset to the bodice waistline.

Vest Variations

The vest may be stitched as a separate garment using faux suede or felt. Follow the cutting instructions on the vest pattern piece V to make a front-closing vest.

Scoop Neckline and Attached Vest (Intermediate; not recommended for 7½- to 8-inch doll)

Use pattern pieces B1 (BF1 and BB1 for a 12-inch doll) and V. First, prepare the basic bodice (see pages 54-55). With right sides facing, stitch the vest fabric to the vest lining, around the neckline, down the center front and across the lower edges, front and back. The neckline of the vest may be cut lower or reshaped for various design applications. Clip the curves, turn the vest right side out and press.

Place the lined vest on the bodice, aligning the armhole edges and side seams. Baste the armhole and side-seam edges together.

Attach the sleeves, then stitch the underarm and side seams. Note: When attaching the bodice to the skirt, be careful not to catch the lower edges of the vest in the waistline seam. To finish, fold the center-back vest facings under and secure them with snaps or tack them to the bodice back.

Square Neckline with Gathered Lace and Vest (Advanced)

Prepare the basic bodice B2 (BF2 and BB2 for a 12-inch doll). Cut a piece of light-weight lace approximately 2½ times the length of the neckline opening. The lace should be wide enough (½-inch to 1¼ inches depending on the doll size) to fall below the bust line of the doll. Run a gathering stitch along the upper and lower edges of the lace. Gently gather the lace, fitting it to the bodice neckline. Pin and then stitch both edges of the lace in

Place the lined vest on top of the basic bodice; the lower vest edges should be ¼-inch above the lower edge of the bodice front and back, exposing the waistline seam allowance. Baste the vest to the bodice.

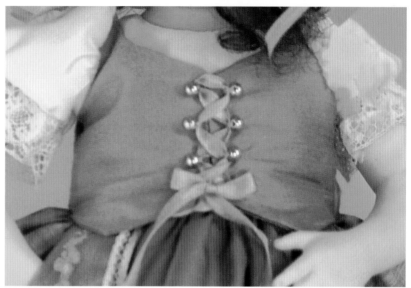

Don't stitch the lower edge of the vest into the waistline seam.

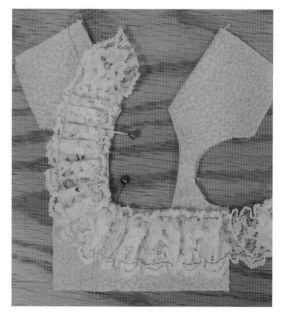

Pin the gathered lace to fit the neckline.

place. Stitch the lace around the armhole and trim the excess lace from the armhole edge.

To cut the vest, place the center front of the vest pattern V on the fold. Cut the vest neckline following the cutting line for felt or faux suede. Prepare the vest similarly to the basic bodice and then baste or pin it in place (see instructions for scooped neckline and attached vest on page 57). The vest may be shortened to fit a shortened bodice. Baste the lower edges of the bodice and vest together before attaching the skirt or sleeves.

Dropped-Waist Bodice

Use pattern B3 (BF3 and BB3 for a 12-inch doll). This pattern is designed as a fitted ballerina-type bodice, and is suitable for stretch fabric. It may be necessary to extend the side seams or back edge for fabrics without stretch.

Before you begin, measure the doll's hips and compare them to the lower edge of the dropped-waist bodice pattern. Make necessary adjustments on the lower side seams, equally adjusting the front and back pattern edges. The hipline should be loose enough to allow room for the skirt's seam allowance. See Instructions for Adjusting Patterns on page 68, if necessary. Follow the basic bodice construction guidelines on pages 54-55.

Sleeve Variations

These various sleeve styles have been designed to accommodate different fabrics. Use the cap sleeve SL1 or the puff sleeve SL5 patterns for sheer, slippery or very fine fabric. Since these fabrics are often hard to handle, the folded lower edge provides for an easy and clean finished hem. Cottons or lightweight tightly woven fabrics, such as taffeta, should be used be used for sleeve patterns SL2, SL3 and SL4.

Gathered Cap Sleeve S1

To create a double-layered cap sleeve, fold the sleeve fabric in half and run two rows of gathering stitches along the sleeve's cap. Gather the sleeve to fit the armhole edge.

Stitch the sleeve to the basic bodice, with right sides facing.

To decorate the cap sleeve, stitch trims to the sleeve before gathering and stitch-

Trim the excess lace from the armhole edge.

Layer the vest, on the bodice, over the gathered lace.

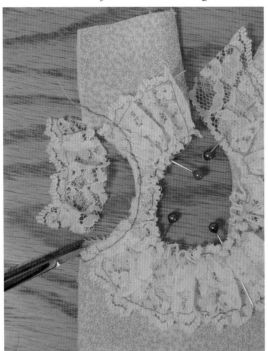

ing it to the bodice. For a soft gathered effect, hand-tack small pleats together on the sleeve fold; to ensure the proper fit and alignment, tack the sleeve when the garment is finished and on the doll.

Basic Gathered Sleeve with ¼-inch Cuff

Use patterns S2, S3 or S4. Before you begin, mark the front of each sleeve. Once the sleeves are gathered, it is hard to tell which is the front or back.

Measure the hand, elbow and bicep of the doll. Sometimes the fingers are spread out wider than the finished armhole or sleeve opening, making it difficult to dress the doll. To ensure the cuff or gathering stay will be long enough, add ¾-inch to the largest of the three arm and hand measurements. This will be the cutting measurement for the cuff or gathering stay; it includes the seam allowance and ease.

Cut the cuff 1-inch wide by the length determined above (the larger of the three measurements plus ¾-inch).

Run two rows of gathering stitches on the top and lower edge of the sleeves. Gather the lower edge of each sleeve.

Fold the cuff lengthwise and stitch it, right sides facing, to the lower edge of the sleeve. Serge the unfinished cuff edge for a clean finish on the seam (optional). Refer to the mark that identifies the front of the sleeve. Stitch the sleeve to the appropriate side of the finished bodice.

Adjust the cuff width or material used—lace, trim, piping, or bias-cut fabric—according to the look and style you want to achieve.

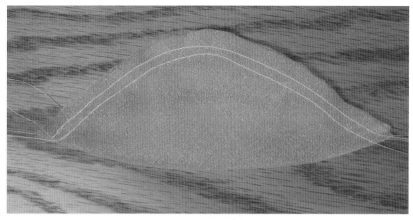

Stitch two rows of gathering stitches on the cap of the sleeve (SL1).

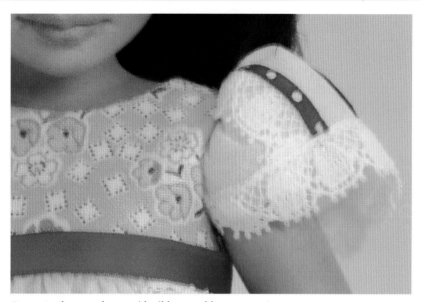

Decorate the cap sleeve with ribbon and lace.

Hand-stitch small pleats on the sleeve fold for a soft gathered effect. Conceal the stitches with a ribbon rose or bow.

Gathered Short Sleeve (SL2) with 1/8-inch cuff. Cut bias cuff 3/4-inch wide.

Gathered Sleeve with Lace and Gathering Stay

Use pattern pieces SL2, SL3 or SL4. When finishing a gathered sleeve with lace, use a gathering stay as an alternative to elastic; the gathering stay will secure the gathers and is not as bulky or as difficult to stitch as elastic.

Before you begin, mark the front of each sleeve with a pin or water-soluble marker. Cut a gathering stay for each sleeve from narrow ribbon or a ½-inch-wide strip of bias-cut fabric. (See the basic gathered-sleeve instructions on page 59 to determine length).

Stitch flat lace to the lower edge of the sleeve, right sides facing. Gather the lower sleeve edge to fit the gathering stay.

Fold the gathering stay lengthwise. To secure the gathers, stitch the gathering stay, close to the folded edge, across the gathered lace seam line. Turn the gathering stay under, like a facing.

Puff Sleeve S5 (Intermediate)

Use pattern piece S5 with sheer ribbon, tulle or lightweight sheer fabric. The gathers on the puff sleeve are secured with a concealed gathering stay or an exposed lace or trim.

Measure for a gathering stay as described in the basic gathered-sleeve instructions on page 59. Cut the gathering stay from a ½-inch-wide bias strip of the

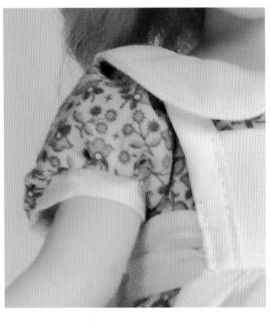

Gathered Medium Sleeve (SL3) with 3/8-inch cuff. Cut straight cuff 1¼-inch wide.

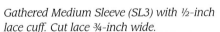

Gathered Medium Sleeve (SL3) with ½-inch lace cuff. Cut lace ¾-inch wide.

Turn the gathering stay under, like a facing

Use a pin to mark the front of each sleeve. Stitch flat lace to the lower edge of the sleeve. Gather the sleeve and lace together. Secure the gathers by stitching a folded bias-cut gathering stay along the gathered edge.

Use ribbon as a gathering stay.

sheer sleeve fabric or from lace or trim.

First, run a gathering stitch down the center of the puff sleeve fabric. Gather it to the length of the gathering stay. Stitch the gathering stay (or the lace or trim) across the sleeve gathers.

To complete the sleeve, fold the sleeve fabric lengthwise, either concealing the gathering stay or exposing the trim (cuff), and align the top edges; run two rows of gathering stitches along the top edge of the puff sleeve, stitching through both layers. Gather and stitch the sleeve to the bodice armhole edge, with right sides facing. Stitch the underarm and side seams, with right sides facing.

Skirt Variations

Basic Gathered Skirt

The gathered skirt S1 is full and best suited for the dirndl effect; follow the cutting guidelines on the pattern piece and the Cutting Dimensions Guide in the Patterns section for the skirt dimensions. If adding horizontal pleats, cut the fabric 2 to 3 inches longer than the desired finished length. Stitch the pleats and the hem before cutting the fabric to its final length. Trim the excess from the top of the skirt fabric; be sure to include a ¼-inch seam allowance. Serge the center back edges or finish the edges with a ¼-inch hem; form facings by pressing the back edges under ½-inch.

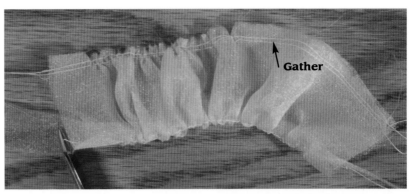

Run a gathering stitch across the top of the sleeve, connecting both sides. Gather the sleeve to fit the bodice armhole edge.

Decorative trim serves as the gather stay, securing the gathers on the outside of the sleeve.

Use pattern S5 for a puff sleeve. Sandwich gathering stay between layers for a soft puffy effect.

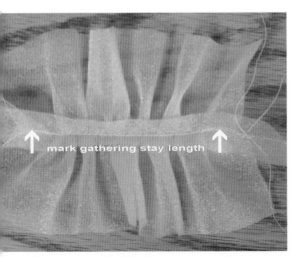

First run a gathering stitch down the center of the puff sleeve fabric. Gather it to the measured length of the gathering stay. Stitch the gathering stay across the sleeve gathers.

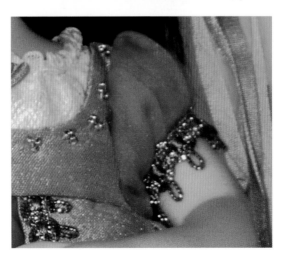

Use trim as the gathering stay for a decorative cuff.

Run two rows of gathering stitches on the top edge of the skirt. Gather the fabric evenly and stitch the skirt to the finished bodice waistline, with right sides facing. Note: Stitch ribbons and other decorations to the skirt fabric before it is gathered. Center the apron or peplums on the bodice and baste them in place before attaching the skirt.

Basic A-line Skirt S2 (Easy)

The A-line skirt offers a full hemline with less gathers at the waist. Use six to eight A-line S2 panels for a skirt. Stitch the panels together, with right sides facing, forming one flat curved piece; leave the back edges open.

Serge the center back edges and fold them under ½-inch to form a facing; press. Gather the waist and stitch the skirt to the finished bodice waistline. To hem, apply lace or piping or stitch a ¼-inch rolled hem.

A-line Modified Panel and Tear-Drop Panel (Intermediate)

The A-line modified panels and the tear-drop panels are stitched in a similar fashion. Cut six to eight panels for a skirt, depending on the desired fullness. The tear-drop panels are lined, so cut an equal number of lining panels.

A-line Modified Panel S3

To begin, lay out all panels side by side. Fold the first panel in half, with right sides facing; stitch one edge and then turn it

Above, left: To make the Basic Gathered Skirt, use pattern piece S1.

Above: Stitch trims to the skirt before gathering it. For accurate positioning, apply ribbon roses after the costume is finished.

Stitch horizontal pleats and hem into the skirt fabric before cutting the final length.

Adjust the hem length according to the costume design. Use a purchased ruffled edging for a designer-look finish.

Hem A-line skirts with narrow piping.

right side out and press the stitched edge. This will be the center back finished edge.

With right sides facing, sandwich the second panel around the first, aligning the raw edges. Stitch the remaining raw edge from the first panel to the second panel. Turn the second panel right side out and press. Repeat this process for the remaining panels.

Stitch decorative trim to the panels before gathering the skirt. Serge the final edge, or stitch a ¼-inch hem and turn it under ½-inch to form a facing. Run two rows of gathering stitches along the top edge. Evenly gather the waist and stitch the skirt to the finished bodice waistline.

Tear-Drop Panel S2

With right sides facing, stitch only the bottom curved edge of each tear-drop panel to a lining panel; the lining may be cut from the same fabric. Clip the curves, turn the pieces right side out and press the curves. After pressing, turn all of the panels inside out to complete the stitching. Stitch the panels together and complete the panels in the same manner as the A-line modified skirt panels.

Tear-Drop Panel with Exposed Underskirt

To create an exposed underskirt, follow the gathered-slip instructions below, using an outer fabric for the lower ruffle. First, stitch the finished tear-drop skirt to the finished bodice waistline. Then gather the waistline of the exposed underskirt

Stitch one edge; this will be the center-back finished edge.

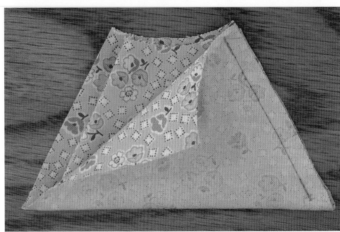

Sandwich the second panel around the first panel and stitch the remaining raw edge.

Stitch the remaining panels using the same process.

Stitch the trim to the A-line modified panels before gathering the waist of the skirt.

For easier sewing, remove the beads that run close to all seam lines. After the costume is finished, replace the beads that are obviously missing.

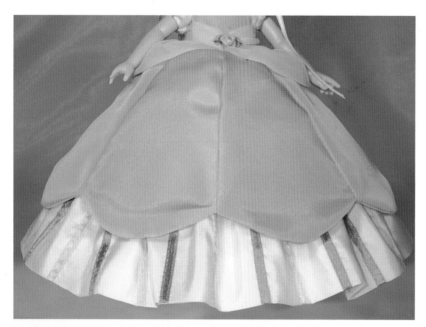

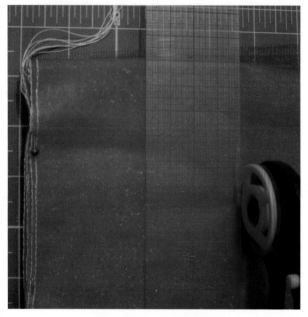

Here is the tear-drop skirt with exposed underskirt.

Use a clear ruler and rotary cutter to trim the tulle.

and stitch it to the finished bodice and skirt waistline. Hem the exposed underskirt after fitting it for length. Note: Full skirts need to be longer than expected, so pin or baste the underskirt to the waistline before trimming any excess length.

Peplum

Cut peplums on the bias. Gather the top edge to fit one half of the finished bodice. Stitch or baste peplums in place before attaching the skirt. See the gathered-cap sleeve instructions for gathering directions.

Tulle Slip

Tulle and illusion can be difficult to handle, but try this approach for easy assembly and beautiful results. Note the finished cut length and width suggested in the Cutting Dimensions Guide in the Patterns section. The tulle will be folded in half so this measurement represents twice the finished length. Cut the tulle at least 2 inches longer than suggested: it will be trimmed to length later. For instance, a 4-inch skirt has a suggested finished cutting length of 8 inches, since it will be folded in half. To allow for sewing and trimming differentials, add at least 2 inches and cut the tulle 10 inches long.

Run a gathering stitch down the center of the tulle, doubling the layers if you want a four-layer slip. Fold the tulle along the stitching line.

Run a second row of gathering stitches ¼-inch away from the fold. Fold the tulle, widthwise, into four sections. Pin along the stitched edge to keep the folds aligned.

Use a clear ruler and a rotary cutter to cut it to the desired/suggested finish length.

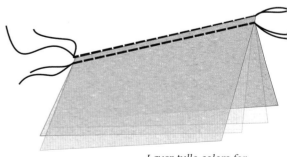

Layer tulle colors for distinctive color palettes.

To gather the tulle, pull both of the bobbin threads from the two rows of gathering stitches. Stitch the tulle slip to the skirt-side of the finished skirt and bodice waist-line. Stitch very close to the folded edge to eliminate extra bulk at the waist.

Gathered or Ruffled Slip

Cut the slip pieces according to the Cutting Dimensions Guide in the Patterns section. Gather the lower ruffle (optional) and stitch it to the upper slip. Apply trims, lace or pleats before checking for the hem length and trimming the top or lower ruffle edge.

Serge or hem the center back edges and then fold the edges under ½-inch to form facings. Determine the finished length and trim the length of the slip, if necessary. Gather the top edge of the slip and stitch it to the finished bodice and skirt waistline.

Aprons

The approach to constructing aprons is very subjective. Depending on the fabric and trim application you choose, the process varies. You may use a fray block product on all outer edges of the apron and trim it with a lace or braid. This keeps the bulk from turned hems to a minimum for a smoother finish. (This is not recommended for doll clothes that will be washed often.)

In one construction method, begin by applying trims or lace to the apron bib and/or apron skirt. Stitch the straps to the apron bib. Gather the apron skirt at the waist, and stitch it to the apron bib, with right sides facing. Apply a fray block product to outer unfinished edges. Stitch a finishing lace or trim to the apron and bib straps edges. Tack the straps to the bodice-back waistline, or stitch them into the waistline seam. Finally, attach the waist ties.

To make the apron bib and strap combination A3, cut two. With right sides facing, stitch along the neckline edge. Clip the curve and turn. Finish the apron as suggested above.

Pantaloons P1, P2 or P3

Waistlines and hips vary from doll to doll. Pre-measure the waist and hips of your doll before cutting the fabric. Compare the measurements to the pattern and adjust the pattern accordingly. (See Instructions for Adjusting Patterns on page 68, if necessary.)

To construct the pantaloons, first stitch the center front seam. Apply lace or trim to straight-leg pantaloons (P1), including ruffles, and/or lace or trim to the full and very full pantaloons (P2 &P3).

Cut decorative ruffle pieces for straight-leg pantaloons from lace or fabric. Cut the ruffle's width twice the width of the pattern's lower-leg-edge; if fabric is used, allow enough length to include a ¼-inch rolled hem and a ¼-inch seam allowance, cutting it at least ¾-inch longer than the desired finished length. Stitch the ruffle's trims and hem before gathering the ruffle and stitching it to the pantaloon leg.

Treat the lower edges of the full and very full pantaloons like the lower edges of the sleeves. Measure the ankle (around the ankle and heel, like an elbow) and calf to determine the length of the gathering stay or cuff and add ¾-inch to allow for seam allowance and ease. (See the Basic Gathered Sleeve with ¼-inch Cuff instructions.)

Ease the waist fullness with a gathering stitch to fit the waist and/or hip measurement, choosing the larger measurement plus ¾-inch for seam allowance and ease. Stitch a folded bias-cut waistband to the pantaloon waistline with right sides facing. Stitch the center back seam. Stitch the pantaloon inseam.

Secure the fit with a snap, hook and eye, or insert a drawstring ribbon through the waistband and secure the fit with a bow.

Hats, Hoods and Capes

Hat or Hood H2 and H4

Use hat or hood H2 and H4 pattern pieces. Fold the hat ruffle along the fold line and stitch on a trim, if desired. Stitch

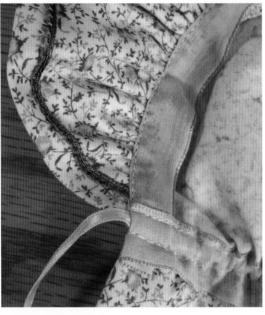

Use lightweight ribbon for the hat facing and to form a casing for the ribbon ties.

Conceal the unfinished seams of the hat with a ribbon or hem tape casing.

Use a folded strip of bias-cut fabric for the hat or hood facing and gathering stay on the cape neckline. Use the gathering stay as a casing for the ribbon ties.

the ruffle to the hat, using a gathering stitch; run a second row of gathering stitches close to the first row.

Gather the front of the hat to fit the hat facing. (See the Cutting Dimensions Guide in the Patterns section.) Stitch the facing, right sides facing, to the ruffle side of the hat and topstitch. Next, fold under the facing on the back of the hat with right sides facing and stitch the side edges; turn and press.

Stitch a casing over the raw edge of the facing, using a lightweight ribbon or hem tape; fold the raw ends of the casing under ½-inch. Insert a ribbon through the casing and fit the hat to the doll. Secure the ribbon on each side of the casing.

Hat or Hood with Straight Cape H2, H4 and Cape

To begin, stitch the ruffle to the hood, according to the hat or hood instructions above. For the cape dimensions, see the Cutting Dimensions Guide in the Patterns section.

Stitch the cape fabric to the cape lining fabric, right sides facing, along the side seams and the lower edge. Turn the cape right sides out and press. Run a gathering stitch across the neckline edge of the cape and fit it to the neckline edge of the hat. With right sides facing, use a gathering stitch to sew the cape to the hat.

Gather the neckline to fit the doll. Complete the cape and hood with a casing at the neckline; the casing secures the gathers. (See the hat or hood instructions above.) Insert a ribbon tie through the casing to complete the cap and hood. Note: Cape pattern H3 can be used with H2 and H4 as well.

Hood and Cape H1 and H3

Cut the fabric and lining for the cape and hood. Stitch the darts on the cape, hood and lining pieces. Stitch the cape lining to the cape, with right sides facing, along the curved edge; turn the cape right sides out and press. Topstitch the finished edge.

Stitch the hood lining to the hood, right

sides facing, along the straight edge; turn the hood right sides out and press. Topstitch the finished edge.

Run two rows of gathering stitches along the curved edge of the hood. Gather the hood to fit the neckline of the cape. Stitch the cape to the hood, right sides facing, using a gathering stitch. Complete the neckline with a casing and ties. (See instructions for hat and hood with straight cape on page 66.)

Juliet/Ballerina Cap JC

This cap requires approximately 12 inches of crafting wire, depending on the size of your doll, and a piece of buckram or heavy interfacing, approximately 6 inches x 6 inches for a 12-inch doll. Use the cap pattern piece JC to cut the buckram or heavy interfacing.

Fold the buckram in half and stitch several casing rows onto the cap. Insert wire into the rows forming a zigzag pattern. The wire will mold the cap's shape to fit the doll.

The rest of the cap should be stitched by hand or secured with glue. Machine stitching over the wire may cause harm to your sewing machine or needle.

To begin, lay a piece of flat or gathered fabric over the molded cap base. Baste the fabric in place along the outside edges; trim the fabric to fit. Use a fray block product to keep edges neat. Use a quick drying fabric glue to apply decorative lace or trim to the edges; add ribbon streamers to complete the look.

Princess Hat PH

This hat requires a piece of buckram, a stiff interfacing, or 1/8-inch craft foam, measuring approximately 7 inches x 7 inches for a 12-inch doll. Cut a hat base using pattern piece PH from the stiff material you choose. Form a cone with it, and fit it to the dolls head. Secure the shape with quick drying fabric glue or tack it by hand if you are using craft foam. Cut the hat fabric slightly larger than the pattern piece PH (about ½-inch larger on each side).

For a clean finish, fold and press one of the straight edges of the hat fabric under ¼-inch. Attach the hat fabric to the buckram or foam base using fabric glue, layering the folded edge over the other straight edge. Glue or stitch the trims and embellishments in place.

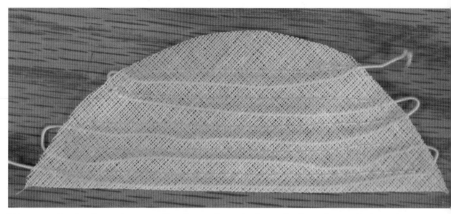

Weave craft wire through rows of casing to form the base for the Juliet/Ballerina Cap.

Form the wired base to fit the doll's head. Hand-stitch fabric to top of the wired cap base. Glue or hand-stitch layers of decorative trims to the outer edges. Finish with streamers and floral accessories.

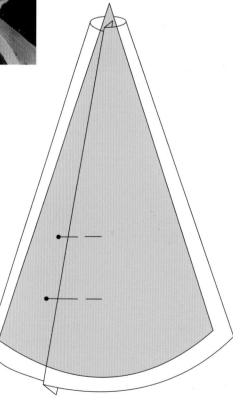

Wrap the hat fabric around the cone shape. Fold one edge under for a neat finish, and then secure it with glue, or stitch it by hand.

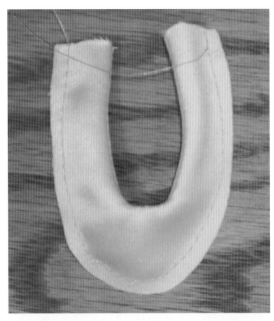

Stitch the lining to the slipper top, turn and press; run a gathering stitch around the outside edge of the slipper.

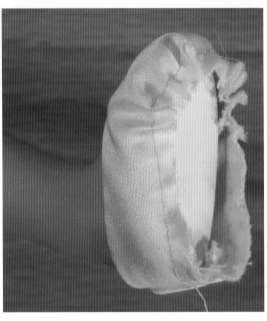

While the slipper is on the doll's foot, glue the slipper top to the inner sole. To conceal the raw edges, glue an outer sole to the slipper bottom.

"First, I see photos, then I sit together with my friend, a designer, and then we try to find a way to work it out. I try to work with three dolls and make their clothes to work together. The fabrics can be silk or cotton, but details are hand done."

—Heidi Plusczok

Ballerina Slippers BSL and SS

Slipper patterns are provided only for 11- and 12-inch dolls. The pattern requires a piece of poster-board-weight cardboard or leather measuring approximately 4 inches x 4 inches for the soles. Cut fabric and lining for each slipper. Stitch the lining to the slipper top along the inner curve, with right sides facing. Turn the fabric right side out, and top stitch the finished edge. Stitch the center back seam, with right sides facing, and then run a gathering stitch around the lower edge of the slipper.

Cut two soles for each slipper from the poster-board-weight cardboard or leather. Choose a color that will complement the slipper. Place the cardboard or leather sole on the foot of the doll. Wrap the slipper around the doll's foot and over the cardboard or leather. Draw the gathers evenly around the toes and heal. Secure the raw edges to the cardboard or leather with quick drying fabric glue.

Glue the remaining cardboard or leather sole to the bottom of the slipper, concealing all of the raw edges. Embellish the slipper with ribbons and trims.

Note: If your storybook character wears socks or tights, make the slipper with the doll's socks or tights on, so that the slipper won't be too small.

Instructions for Adjusting Patterns
Bodice

If the bodice front is too loose at the neckline or across the chest front, move the pattern fold line in slightly, ¼-inch or less. This will make the neckline or neck hole smaller, as well as making the chest narrower, moving the armhole edge in.

If the back is too tight, move the center back seam out, up to ½-inch. There should be enough overlap to accommodate the snap closure, overlapping at least ¼-inch. If the back is too loose, with more than a ½-inch overlap, move the center back seam in slightly 3/8-inch or less, or make the adjustments at the side seams.

If the bodice fits, but is too tight at the

waist or hips, angle the side seams out. A ¼-inch increase at each side seam, front and back, will increase the waist one full inch.

To increase the side seam equally at the chest and waist, extend the entire side seam.

Remember: The bulk from the gathered skirt and slips requires that the bodice fit loosely at the waist before the skirt or slip is attached.

Pantaloons

To increase the waist or hip measurement on pantaloons, cut the pattern and spread it apart the necessary amount. For instance, to increase the waist or hip measurement by 1 inch, spread the pattern sections ½-inch apart. Since there are two pantaloon halves, increasing each side ½-inch will total a 1-inch increase. Tape the separated pieces to a piece of paper.

To lengthen the crotch, cut the pattern and spread it apart the desired amount. Tape the separated pieces to a piece of paper. Redraw the center front and center back cutting lines.

If both the hip/waist and crotch lengths need to be adjusted, consider using a pattern one size smaller or one size larger.

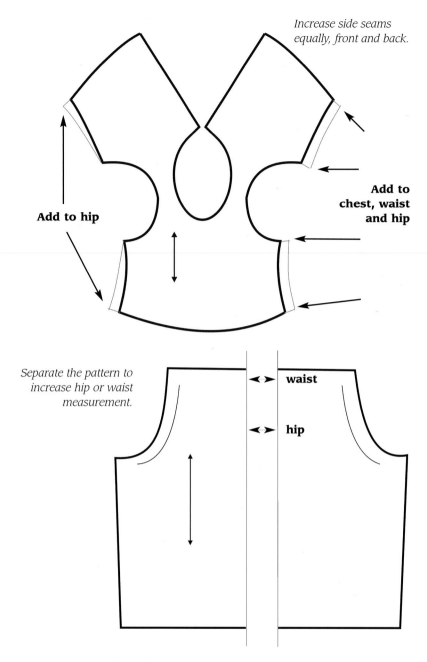

Increase side seams equally, front and back.

Add to hip

Add to chest, waist and hip

Separate the pattern to increase hip or waist measurement.

waist

hip

Increase bodice back width

Move the fold line in slightly to decrease the bodice front width; extend the back edge cutting line to increase the back width.

Decrease bodice front width

The crotch length will vary depending on the girth of the doll. To increase the crotch length, cut the pattern and add the necessary length. Secure the pattern pieces with a strip of paper and tape.

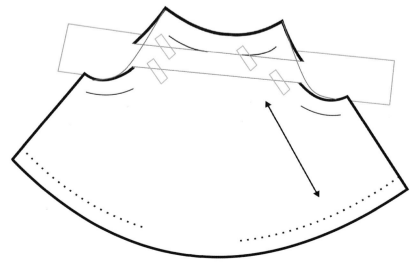

Part III: Patterns

Descriptions of Pattern Pieces

B1 BF1 BB1	Bodice – Scoop Neckline; Front & Back
B2 BF2 BB2	Bodice – Square Neckline; Front and Back
B3 BF3 BB3	Bodice – Dropped Waist; Front and Back
B4	Bodice – V-Shaped Inset
B5	Bodice – Gathered Inset
SL1	Sleeve – Gathered Cap
SL2	Sleeve – Gathered Short
SL3	Sleeve – Gathered Medium
SL4	Sleeve – Gathered Long
SL5	Sleeve – Puffed Sheer
S1	Skirt/Slip – Gathered
S2	Skirt – A-line Panel and Tear Drop
S3	Skirt – A-line Modified Panel
P1	Pantaloons – Straight Leg
P2	Pantaloons – Full
P3	Pantaloons – Very Full
A1	Apron
A2	Apron – Modified Skirt
A3	Apron – Bib and Straps
A4	Apron – Bib
A5	Apron – Straps
H1	Hood
H2	Hat or Hood
H3	Cape
H4	Hat or Hood Ruffle
C	Collar
C1	Corset
P	Peplum
V	Vest
PH	Princess Hat
JC	Juliet/Ballerina Cap
BSL	Ballet Slipper
SS	Ballet Slipper Sole
S	Scarf
SK	Sock

Cutting Dimensions Guide

Example	Pattern Piece	7½" - 8" dolls	10" dolls	11" dolls	12"-13" dolls
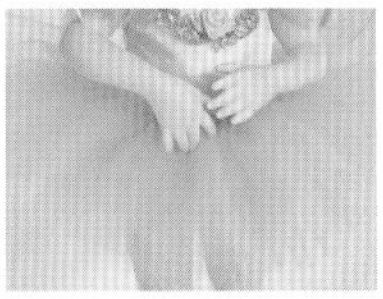	Short Tutu Tulle Slip/ Finished Cutting Length/ see *General Instructions* for details	Finished cut is 3½", folded in half for a finished length of 1¾"	Finished cut is 4½", folded in half for a finished length of 2¼"	Finished cut is 5", folded in half for a finished length of 2½"	Finished cut is 6", folded in half for a finished length of 3"
	Medium Tutu Tulle Slip/ Finished Cutting Length/ see *General Instructions* for details	Finished cut is 6", folded in half for a finished length of 3"	Finished cut is 7", folded in half for a finished length of 3½"	Finished cut is 8", folded in half for a finished length of 4"	Finished cut is 9", folded in half for a finished length of 4½"
	Long Tutu Tulle Slip/ Finished Cutting Length/ see *General Instructions* for details.	Finished cut is 8", folded in half for a finished length of 4"	Finished cut is 10", folded in half for a finished length of 5"	Finished cut is 12", folded in half for a finished length of 6"	Finished cut is 15", folded in half for a finished length of 7½"
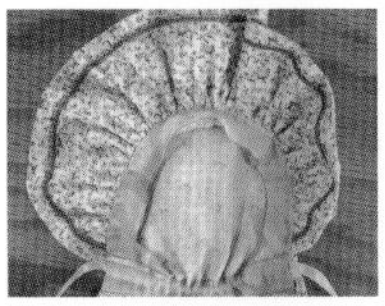	Facing for Hat H2 & H4 Little Bo Peep, and Little Red Riding Hood	Cut bias or ribbon 6" long, or fit to head size	Cut bias or ribbon 6¾" long, or fit to head size	Cut bias or ribbon 7½" long, or fit to head size	Cut bias or ribbon 8½" long, or fit to head size
	Bias Neckline Casing for Hat and Hood Little Red Riding Hood and Little Bo Peep	Gather neckline to 2¾"; cut bias or ribbon 3½" - allow 3/8" to fold under on each end	Gather neckline to 3"; cut bias or ribbon 3¾"- allow 3/8" to fold under on each end	Gather neckline to 3½"; cut bias or ribbon 4¼" - allow 3/8" to fold under on each end	Gather neckline to 4"; cut bias or ribbon 4¾" - allow 3/8" to fold under on each end
	Red Riding Hood Straight-cut Cape	5" long 7½" wide Cut 2	8" long 11" wide Cut 2	9½" long 14" wide Cut 2	10½" long 16 wide Cut 2
	Short skirts Hem length will vary depending on bodice length	Finished length is 2¼", cut skirt at least 3½", to allow for hem and seam; add extra for pleats	Finished length is 3½"; cut skirt at least 5", to allow for hem and seam; add extra for pleats	Finished length is 4¼"; cut skirt at least 6", to allow for hem and seam, add extra for pleats	Finished length is 5"; cut skirt at least 6½" to allow for hem and seam, add extra for pleats
	Tea-length skirts Hem length will vary depending on bodice length	Finished length is 3¼", cut skirt at least 4½" to allow for hem and seam; add extra for pleats	Finished length is 4¼", cut skirt at least 5½", to allow for hem and seam; add extra for pleats	Finished length is 5", cut skirt at least 6½" , to allow for hem and seam; add extra for pleats	Finished length is 6¼", cut skirt at least 7½", to allow for hem and seam; add extra for pleats
	Floor-length Skirts Hem length will vary depending on bodice length	Finished length is 5", cut skirt at least 6" to allow for hem and seam; add extra for pleats	Finished length is 6¼", cut skirt at least 7½" to allow for hem and seam; add extra for pleats	Finished length is 7", cut skirt at least 8½" to allow for hem and seam; add extra for pleats	Finished length is 8", cut skirt at least 9½" to allow for hem and seam; add extra for pleats
	Lace overlay for skirts Length will vary depending on lace width; Measurement given for mid-calf length lace	Cut lace 3" per panel used; for 8 panels, cut lace 24"	Cut lace 4" per panel used; for 8 panels, cut lace 32"	Cut lace 5" per panel used; for 8 panels, cut lace 40"	Cut lace 7" per panel used; for 8 panels, cut lace 56"
	Gathered and Ruffled Slip Measurements for slip and ruffle on a full-length slip or exposed under skirt	Cut upper slip 16" x 3" Cut lower ruffle 30" x 4½" Hem ruffle after fitting on doll	Cut upper slip 18" x 4" Cut lower ruffle 36" x 5½" Hem ruffle after fitting on doll	Cut upper slip 22" X 4½" Cut lower ruffle 40" x 6" Hem ruffle after fitting on doll	Cut upper slip 24" x 5" Cut lower ruffle 45" x 6½" Hem ruffle after fitting on doll

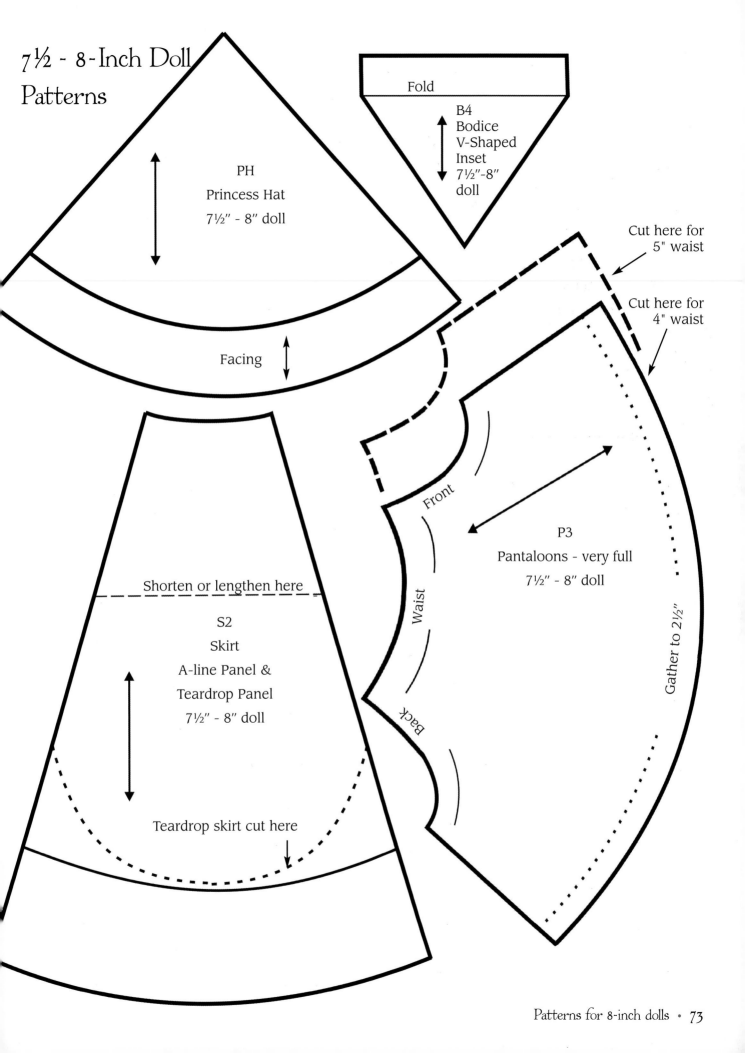

7½ - 8-Inch Doll
Patterns

PH
Princess Hat
7½″ - 8″ doll

Fold

B4
Bodice
V-Shaped
Inset
7½″-8″
doll

Facing

Cut here for
5" waist

Cut here for
4" waist

Front

Waist

Back

P3
Pantaloons - very full
7½″ - 8″ doll

Gather to 2½″

Shorten or lengthen here

S2
Skirt
A-line Panel &
Teardrop Panel
7½″ - 8″ doll

Teardrop skirt cut here

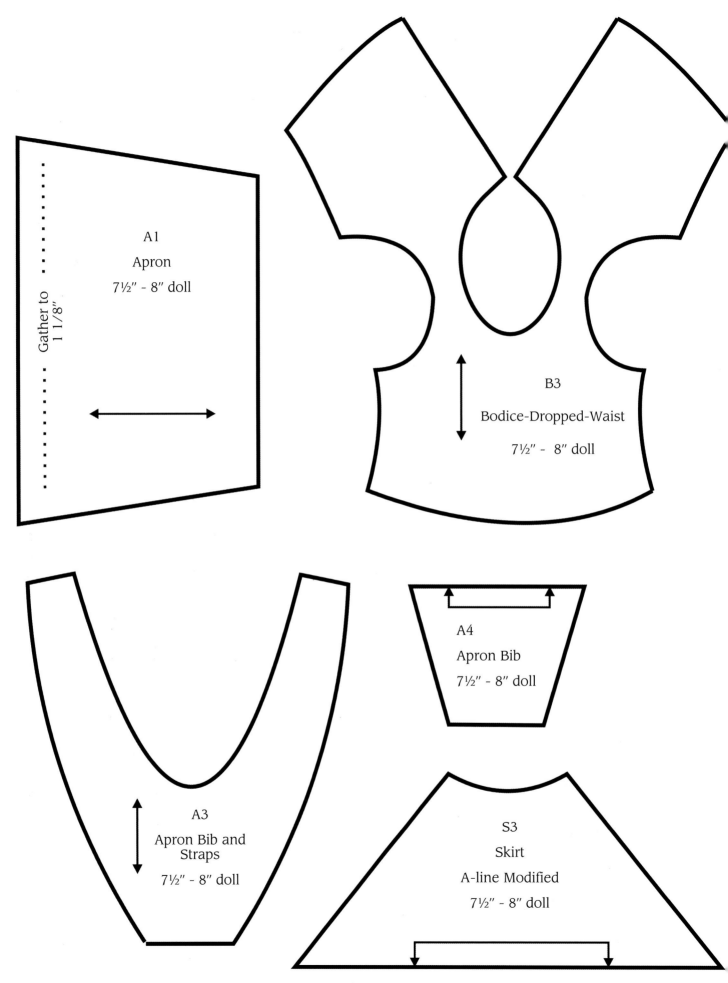

A1
Apron
7½″ - 8″ doll

Gather to 1 1/8″

B3
Bodice-Dropped-Waist
7½″ - 8″ doll

A3
Apron Bib and
Straps
7½″ - 8″ doll

A4
Apron Bib
7½″ - 8″ doll

S3
Skirt
A-line Modified
7½″ - 8″ doll

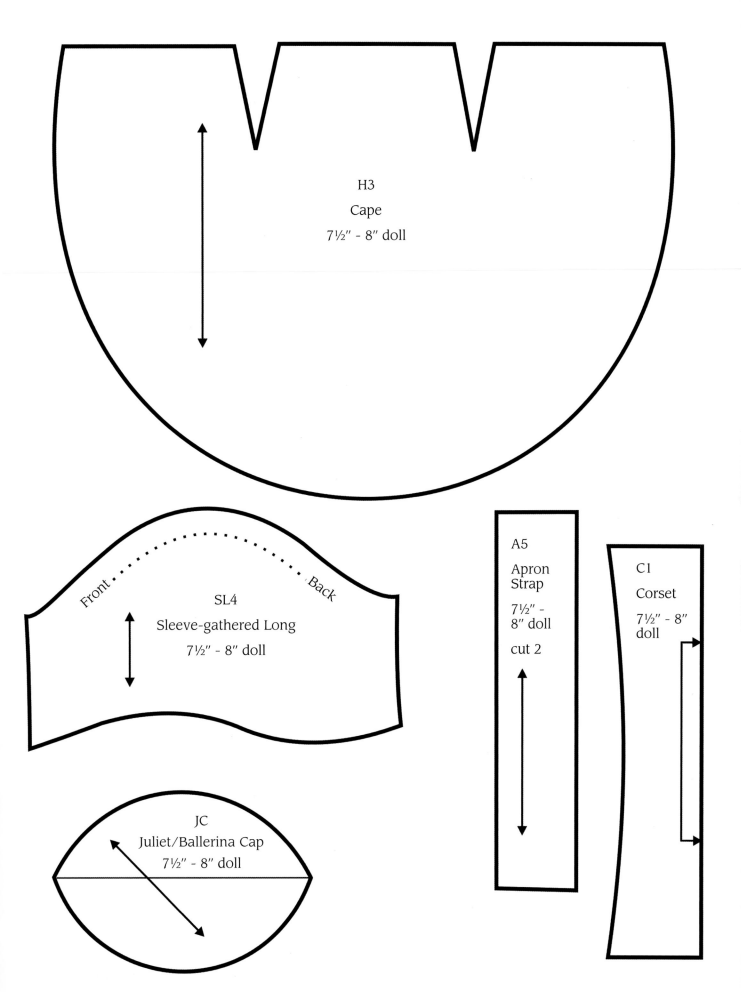

H3
Cape
7½" - 8" doll

SL4
Sleeve-gathered Long
7½" - 8" doll

Front

Back

JC
Juliet/Ballerina Cap
7½" - 8" doll

A5
Apron
Strap
7½" -
8" doll
cut 2

C1
Corset
7½" - 8"
doll

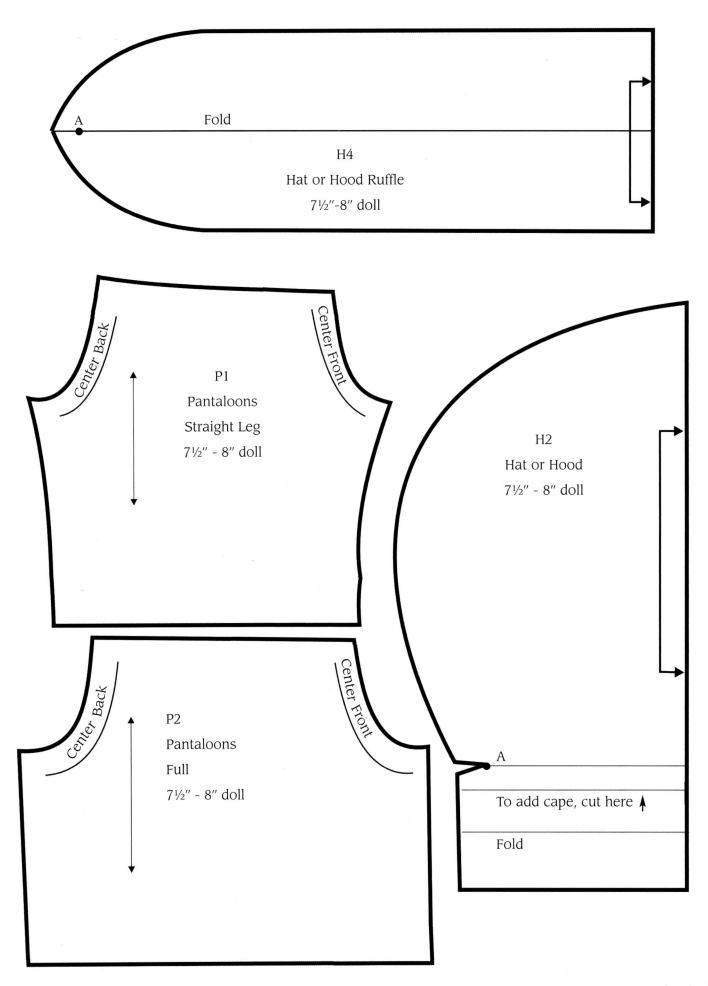

Fold

A

H4
Hat or Hood Ruffle
7½″-8″ doll

Center Back

Center Front

P1
Pantaloons
Straight Leg
7½″ - 8″ doll

H2
Hat or Hood
7½″ - 8″ doll

Center Back

Center Front

P2
Pantaloons
Full
7½″ - 8″ doll

A

To add cape, cut here ↑

Fold

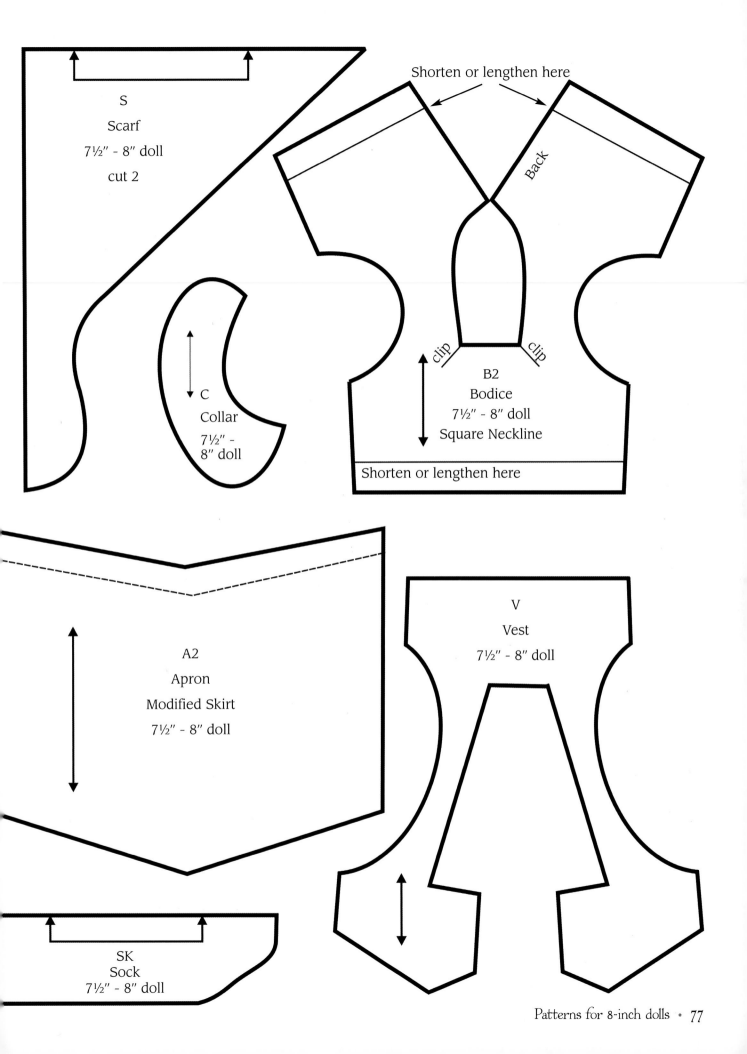

S
Scarf
7½" - 8" doll
cut 2

C
Collar
7½" - 8" doll

Shorten or lengthen here

Back

clip clip

B2
Bodice
7½" - 8" doll
Square Neckline

Shorten or lengthen here

A2
Apron
Modified Skirt
7½" - 8" doll

V
Vest
7½" - 8" doll

SK
Sock
7½" - 8" doll

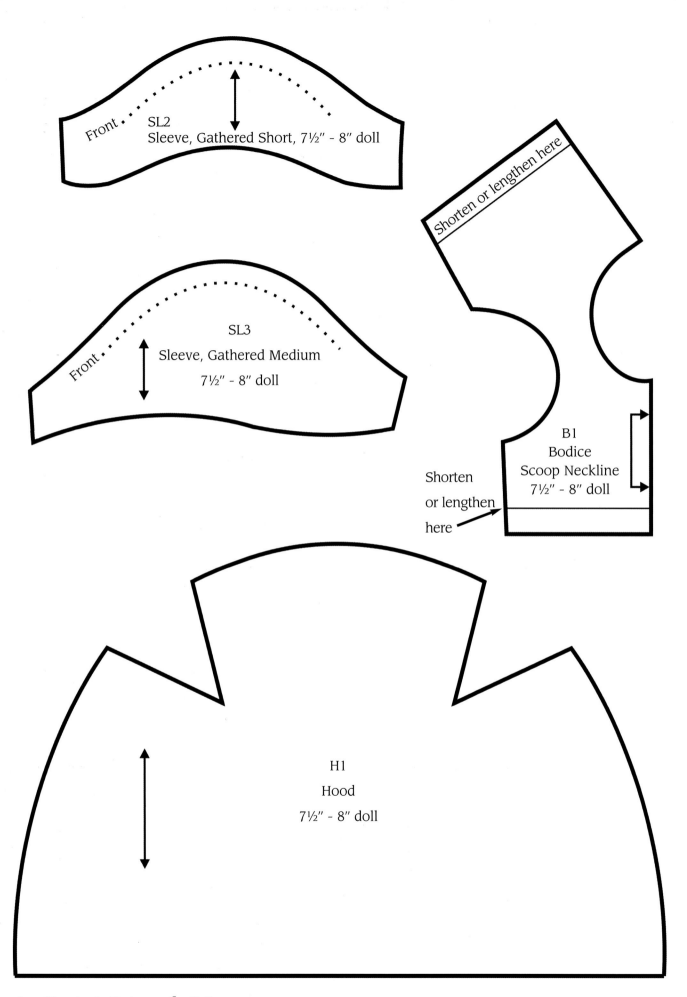

Front · · · SL2
Sleeve, Gathered Short, 7½″ - 8″ doll

Front · · · SL3
Sleeve, Gathered Medium
7½″ - 8″ doll

Shorten or lengthen here

B1
Bodice
Scoop Neckline
7½″ - 8″ doll

Shorten
or lengthen
here

H1
Hood
7½″ - 8″ doll

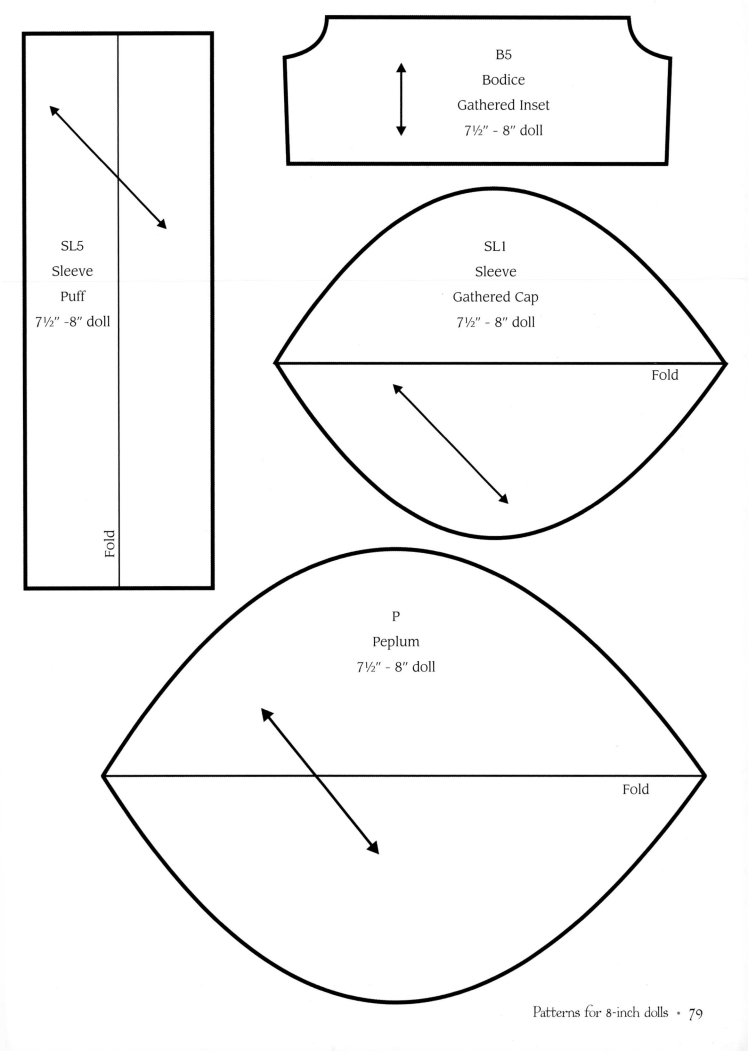

SL5
Sleeve
Puff
7½″ -8″ doll

Fold

B5
Bodice
Gathered Inset
7½″ - 8″ doll

SL1
Sleeve
Gathered Cap
7½″ - 8″ doll

Fold

P
Peplum
7½″ - 8″ doll

Fold

1"
2"
3"
4"
5"
6"

S1
Skirt and Slip
Gathered
7½" - 8" doll

Cut net/tulle slips 24" wide

Cut skirt 16" - 20" wide

See General Instructions and Cutting Dimensions Guide, page 72

10-Inch Doll Patterns

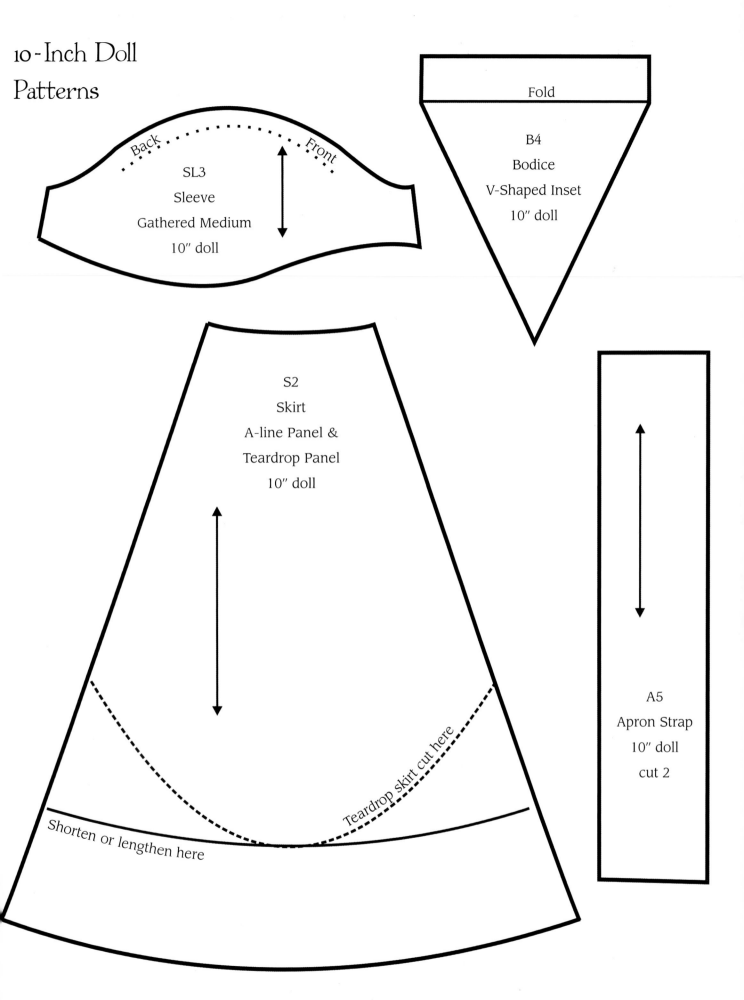

SL3
Sleeve
Gathered Medium
10″ doll

Back

Front

Fold

B4
Bodice
V-Shaped Inset
10″ doll

S2
Skirt
A-line Panel &
Teardrop Panel
10″ doll

Teardrop skirt cut here

Shorten or lengthen here

A5
Apron Strap
10″ doll
cut 2

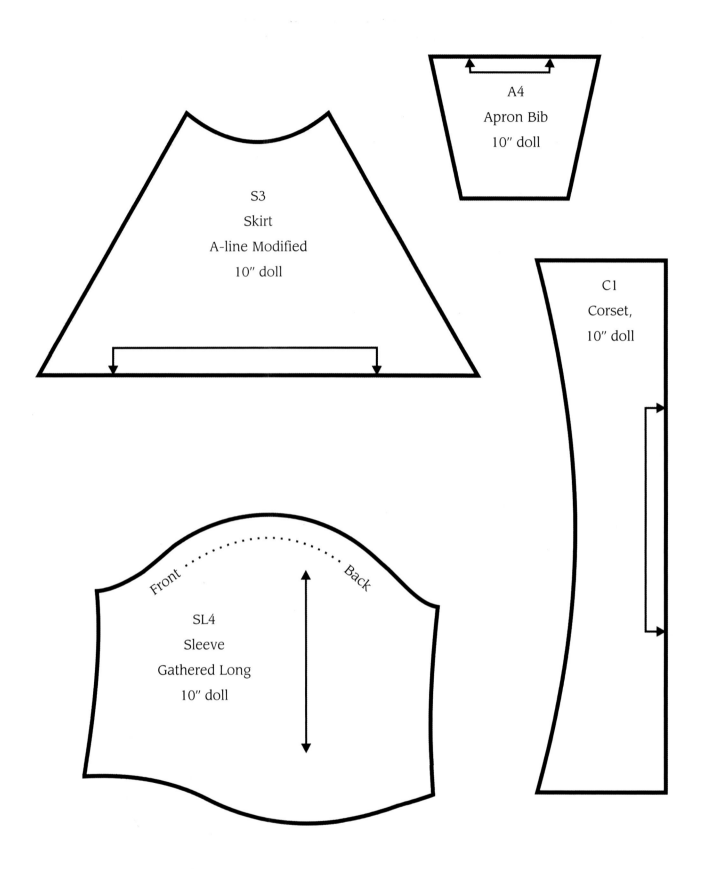

A4
Apron Bib
10″ doll

S3
Skirt
A-line Modified
10″ doll

C1
Corset,
10″ doll

Front · · · · · · · · · · Back

SL4
Sleeve
Gathered Long
10″ doll

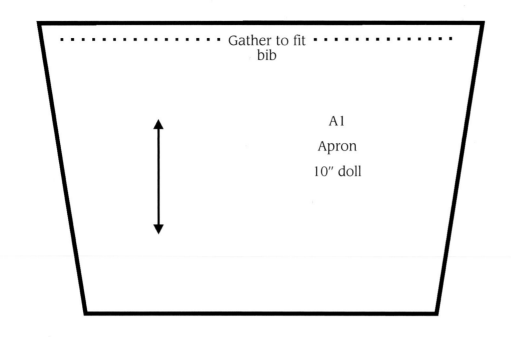

Gather to fit
bib

A1
Apron
10″ doll

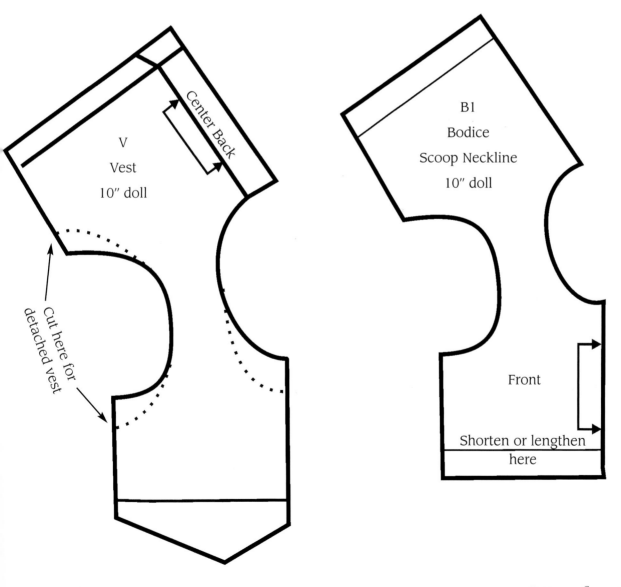

V
Vest
10″ doll

Center Back

Cut here for
detached vest

B1
Bodice
Scoop Neckline
10″ doll

Front

Shorten or lengthen
here

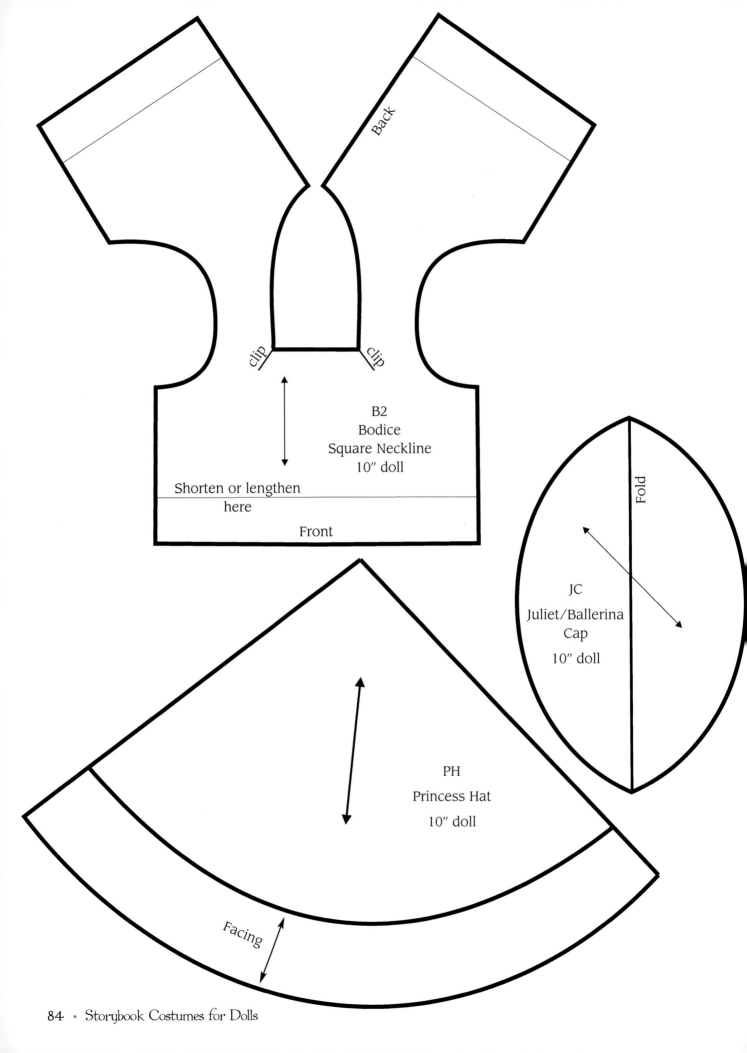

Back

clip   clip

B2
Bodice
Square Neckline
10″ doll

Shorten or lengthen
here

Front

Fold

JC
Juliet/Ballerina
Cap
10″ doll

PH
Princess Hat
10″ doll

Facing

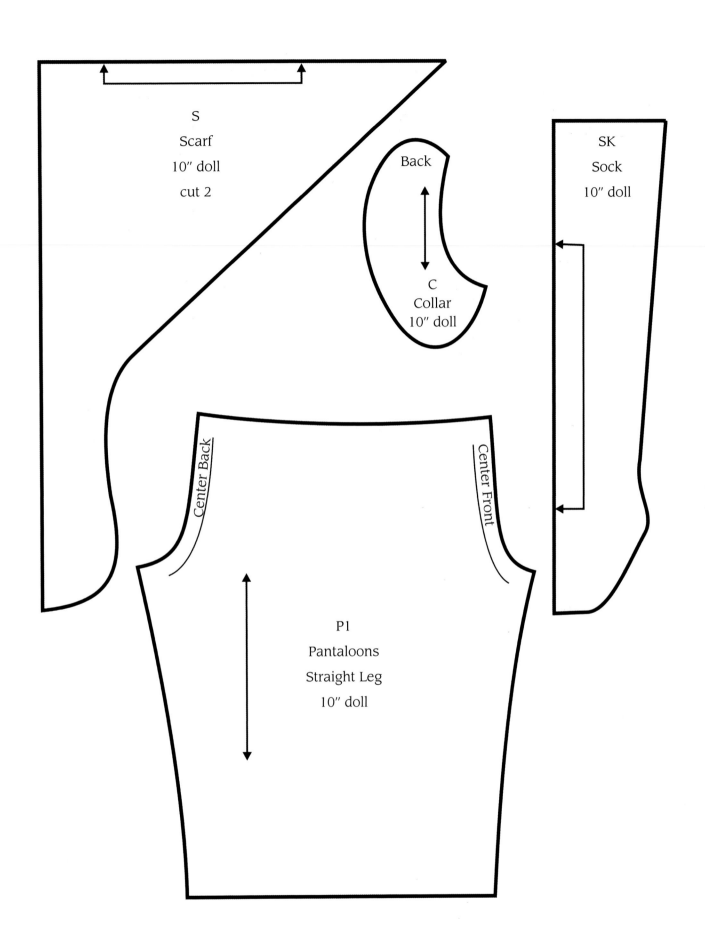

S
Scarf
10″ doll
cut 2

Back

C
Collar
10″ doll

SK
Sock
10″ doll

Center Back

Center Front

P1
Pantaloons
Straight Leg
10″ doll

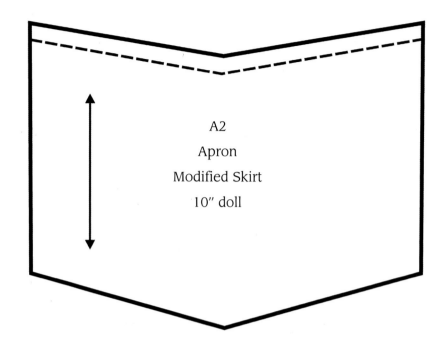

A2
Apron
Modified Skirt
10″ doll

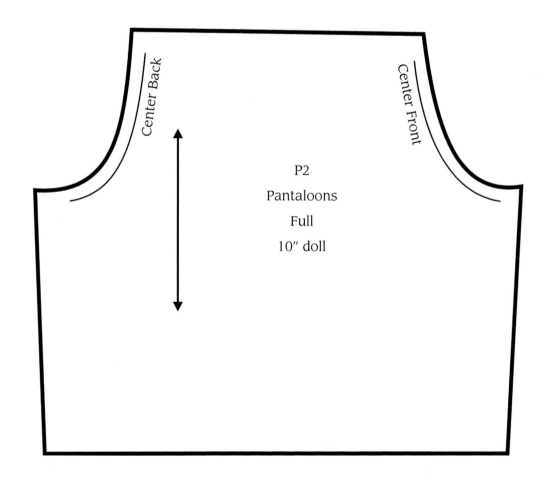

Center Back

Center Front

P2
Pantaloons
Full
10″ doll

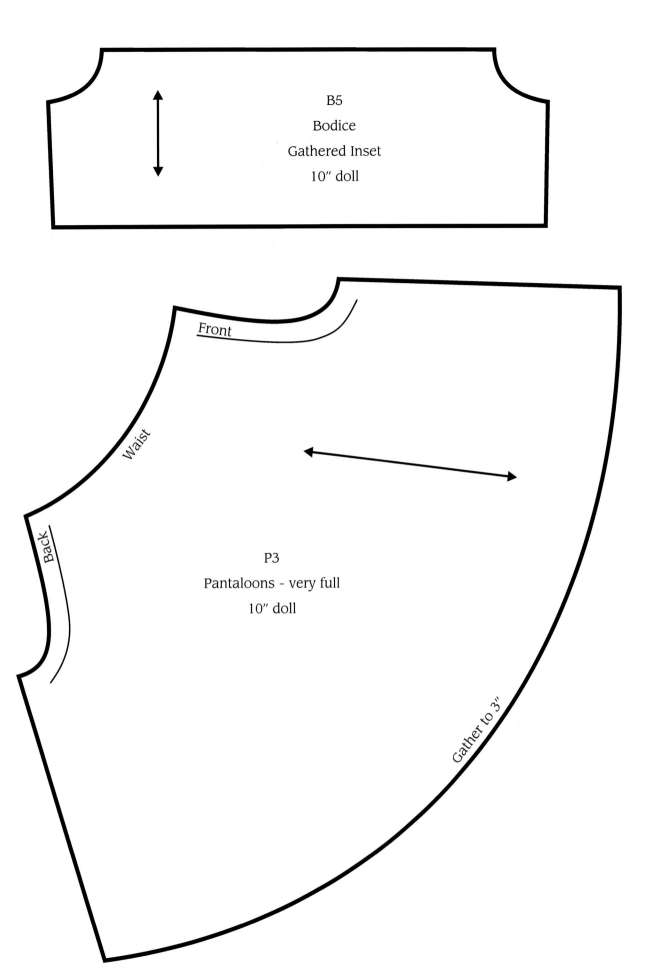

B5
Bodice
Gathered Inset
10″ doll

Front

Waist

Back

P3
Pantaloons - very full
10″ doll

Gather to 3″

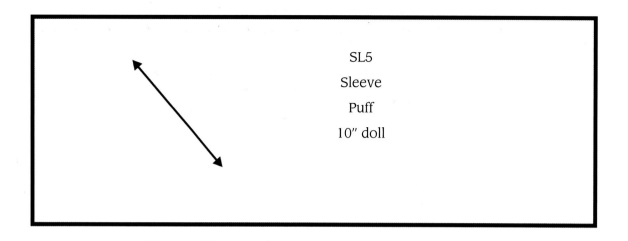

SL5
Sleeve
Puff
10″ doll

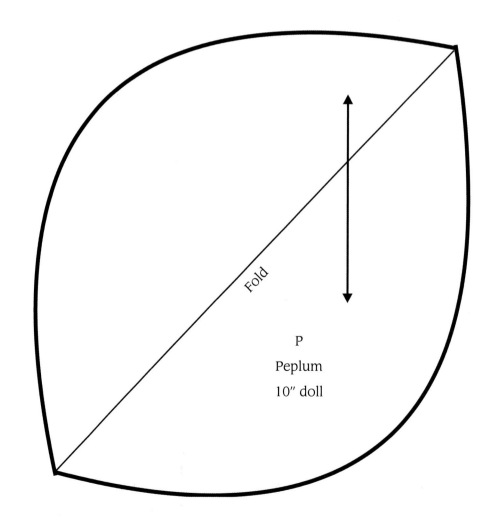

Fold

P
Peplum
10″ doll

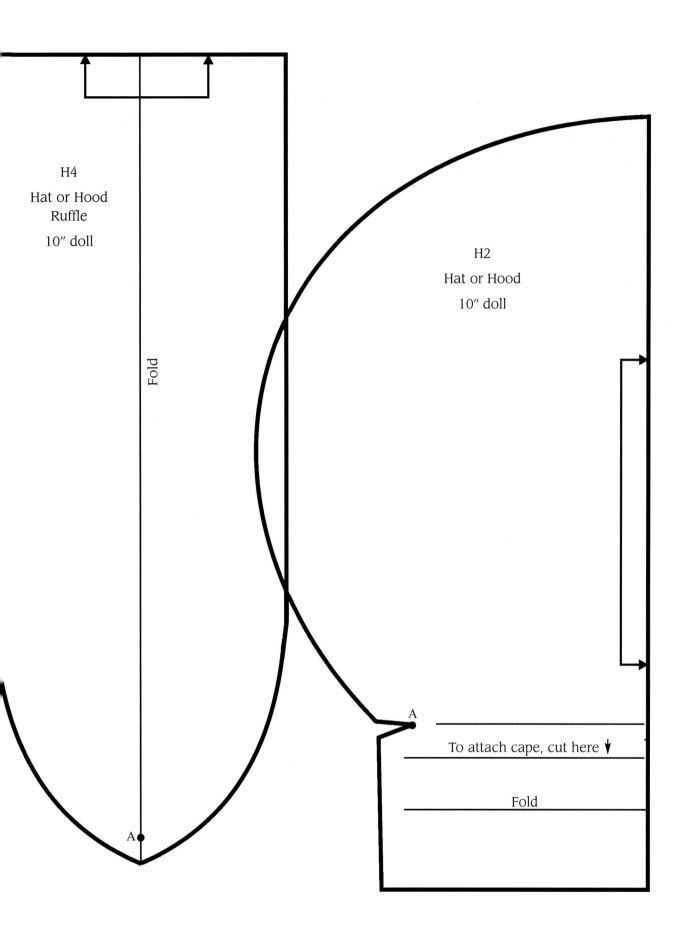

H4
Hat or Hood
Ruffle
10″ doll

Fold

A

H2
Hat or Hood
10″ doll

A

To attach cape, cut here ↓

Fold

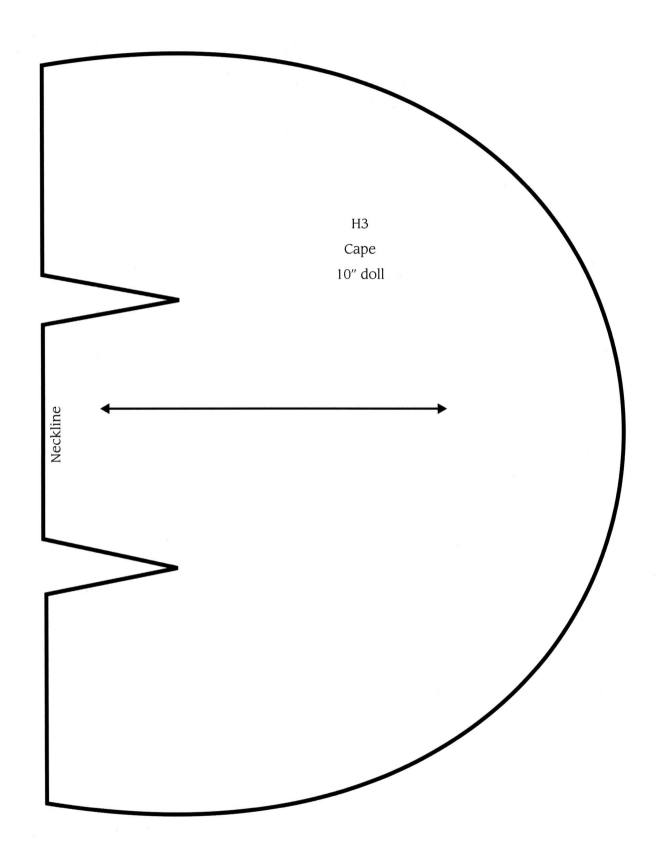

H3
Cape
10″ doll

Neckline

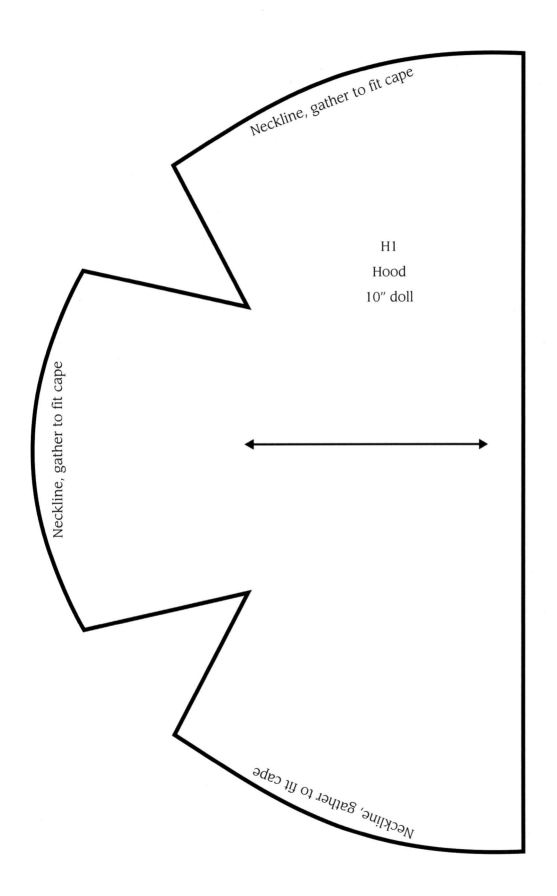

Neckline, gather to fit cape

Neckline, gather to fit cape

Neckline, gather to fit cape

H1
Hood
10″ doll

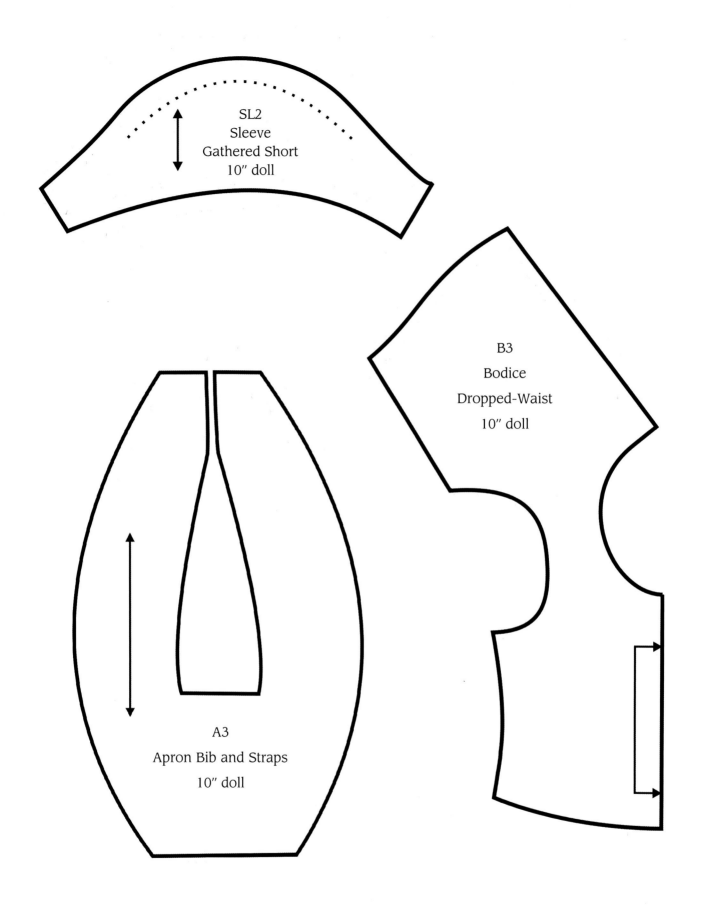

SL2
Sleeve
Gathered Short
10″ doll

B3
Bodice
Dropped-Waist
10″ doll

A3
Apron Bib and Straps
10″ doll

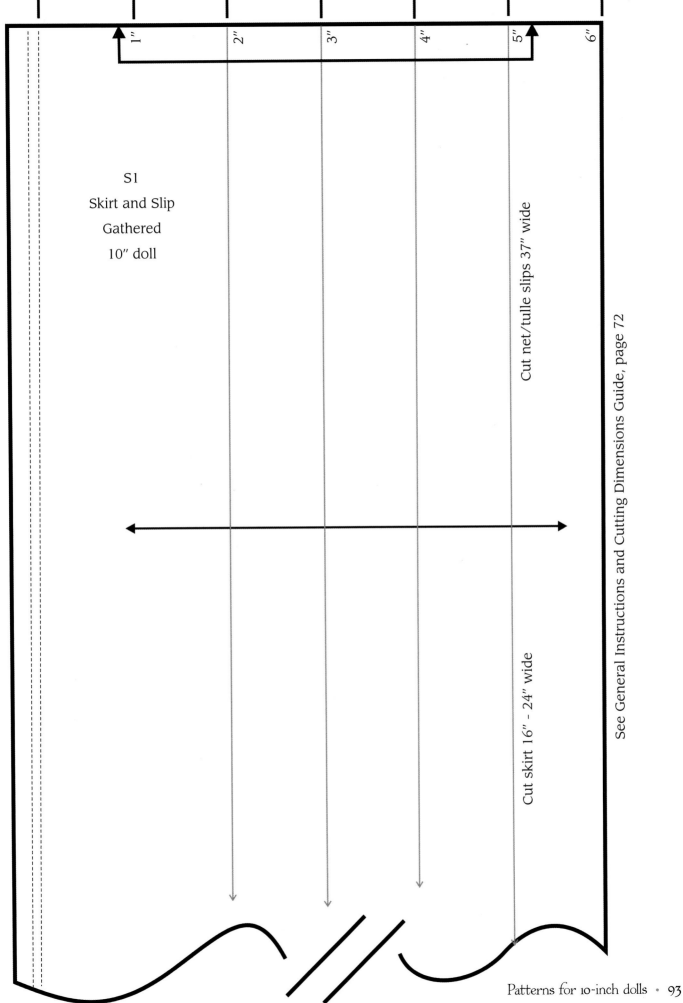

1" 2" 3" 4" 5" 6"

S1
Skirt and Slip
Gathered
10" doll

Cut net/tulle slips 37" wide

Cut skirt 16" – 24" wide

See General Instructions and Cutting Dimensions Guide, page 72

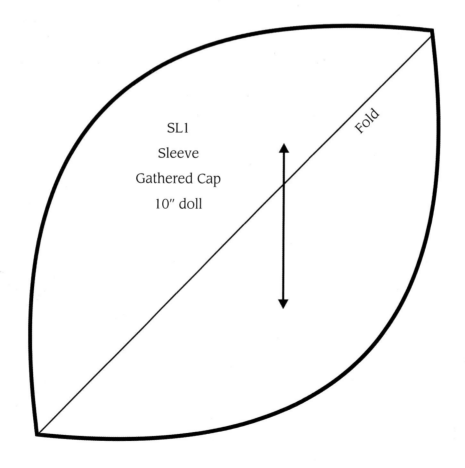

SL1
Sleeve
Gathered Cap
10″ doll

Fold

11-Inch Doll Patterns

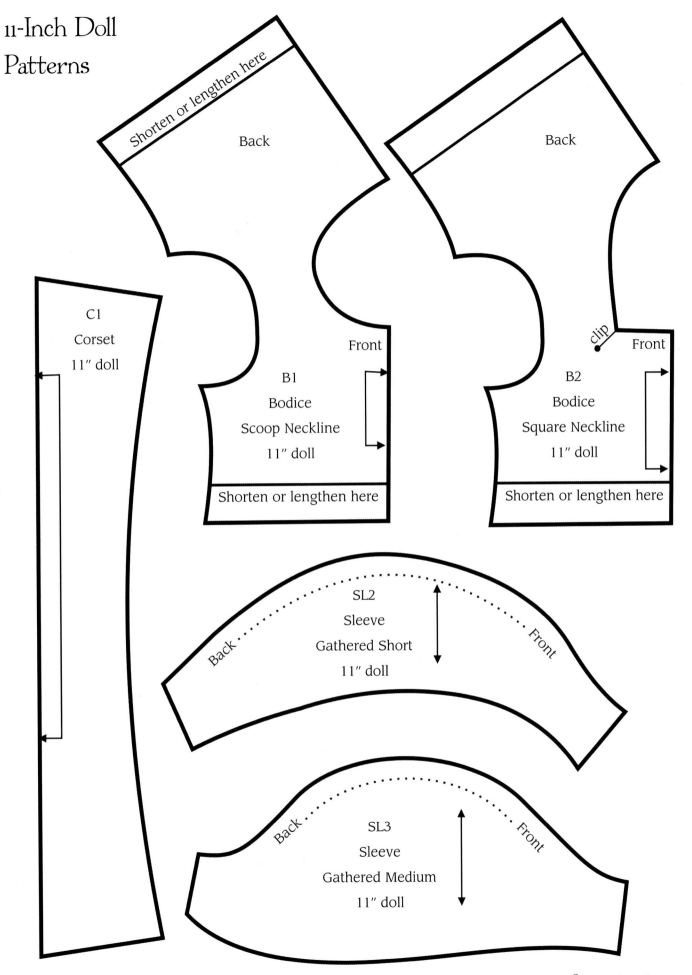

Shorten or lengthen here

Back

Back

C1
Corset
11″ doll

Front

B1
Bodice
Scoop Neckline
11″ doll

Shorten or lengthen here

clip

Front

B2
Bodice
Square Neckline
11″ doll

Shorten or lengthen here

Back

SL2
Sleeve
Gathered Short
11″ doll

Front

Back

SL3
Sleeve
Gathered Medium
11″ doll

Front

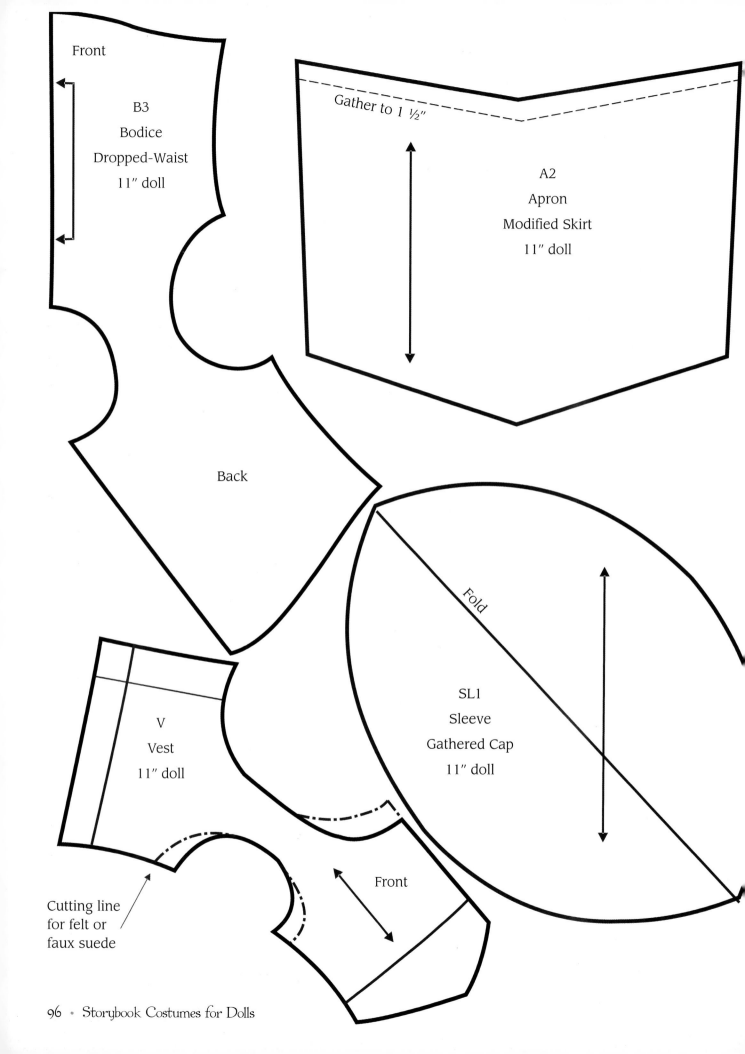

Front

B3
Bodice
Dropped-Waist
11″ doll

Gather to 1 ½″

A2
Apron
Modified Skirt
11″ doll

Back

Fold

SL1
Sleeve
Gathered Cap
11″ doll

V
Vest
11″ doll

Cutting line
for felt or
faux suede

Front

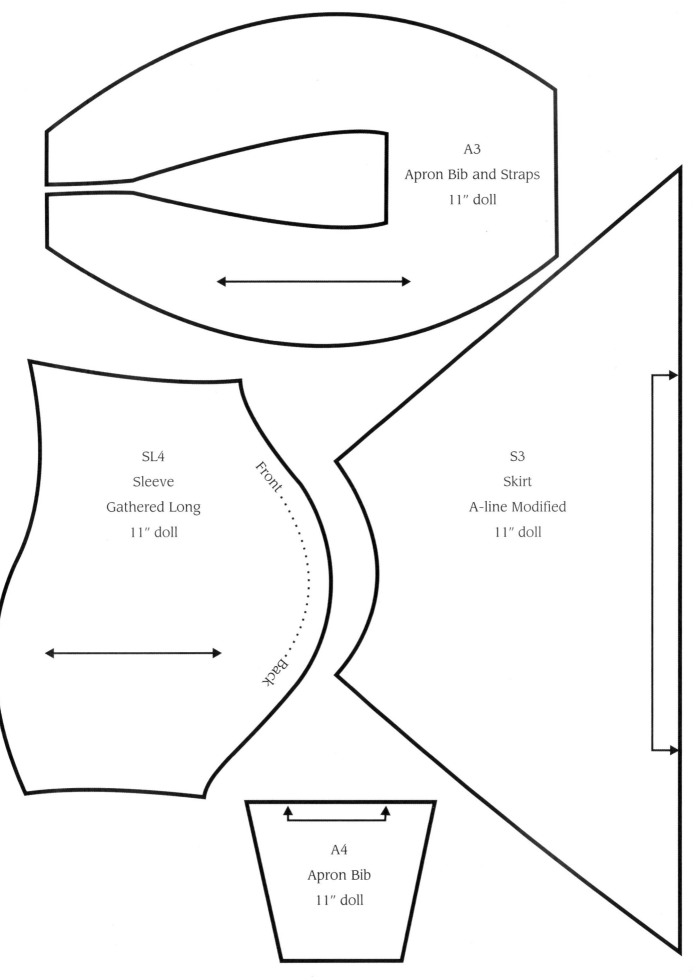

A3
Apron Bib and Straps
11" doll

SL4
Sleeve
Gathered Long
11" doll

Front

Back

S3
Skirt
A-line Modified
11" doll

A4
Apron Bib
11" doll

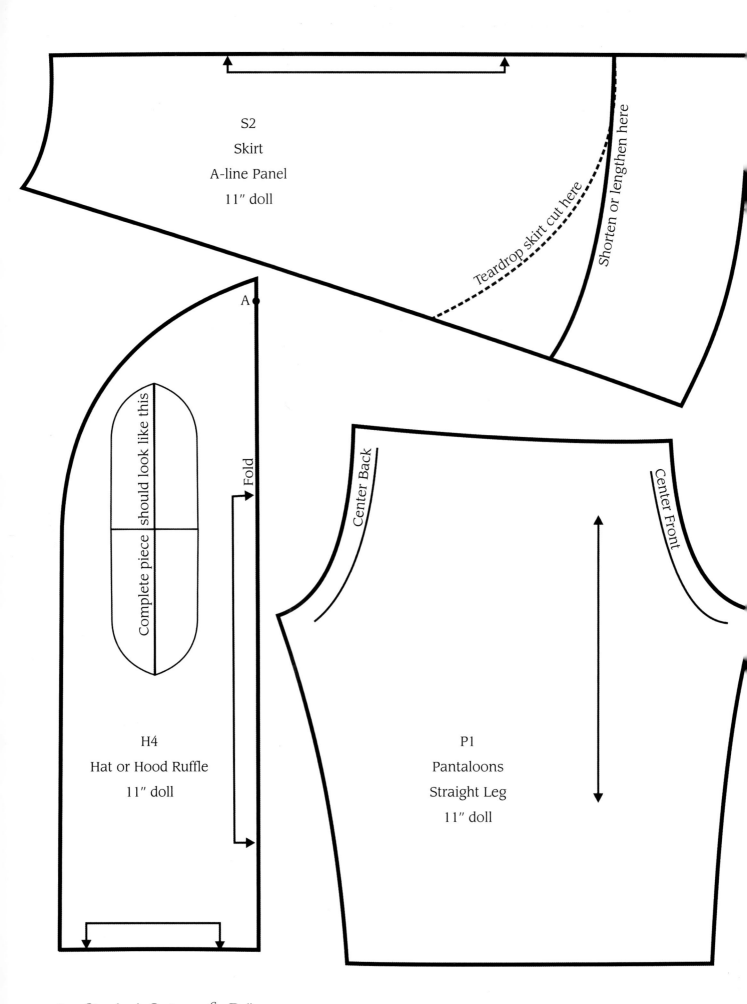

S2
Skirt
A-line Panel
11″ doll

Teardrop skirt cut here

Shorten or lengthen here

A

Fold

Complete piece should look like this

H4
Hat or Hood Ruffle
11″ doll

Center Back

Center Front

P1
Pantaloons
Straight Leg
11″ doll

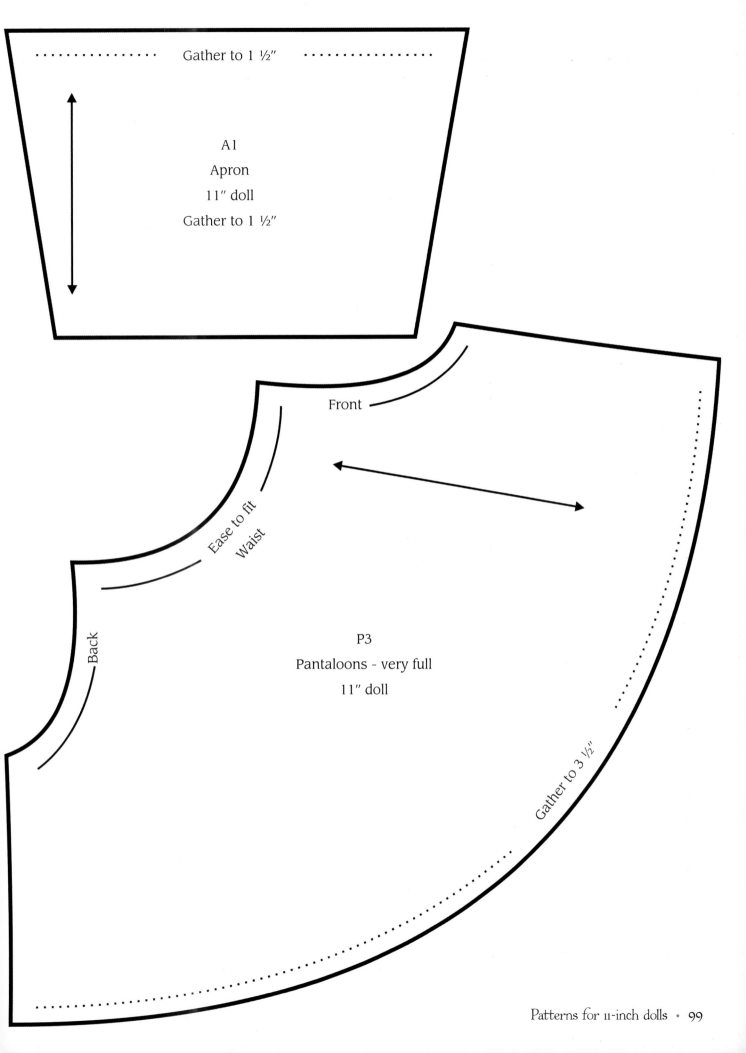

Gather to 1 ½"

A1
Apron
11" doll
Gather to 1 ½"

Front

Ease to fit

Waist

Back

P3
Pantaloons - very full
11" doll

Gather to 3 ½"

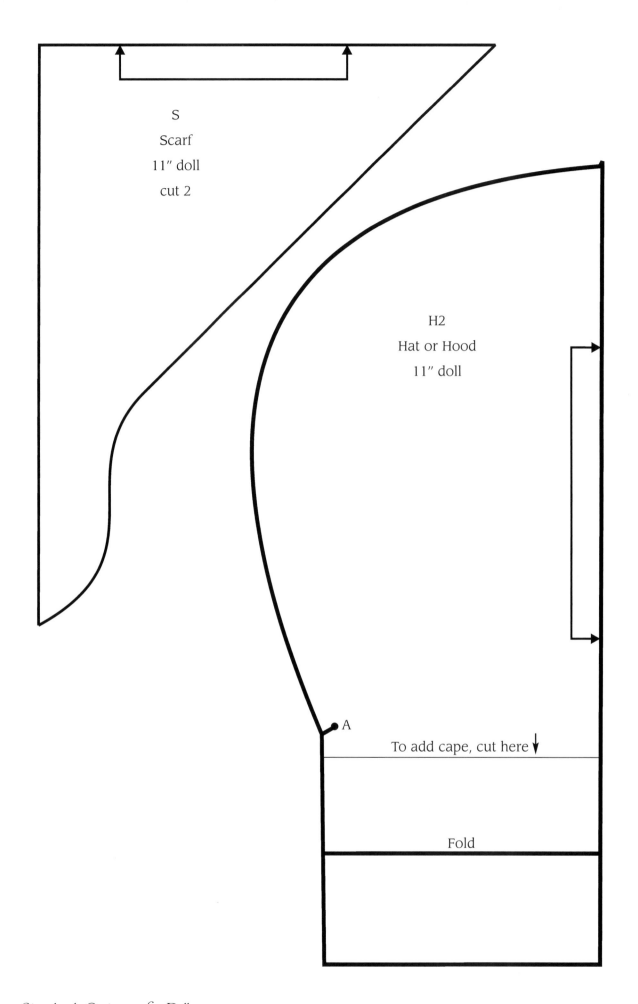

S

Scarf

11″ doll

cut 2

H2
Hat or Hood
11″ doll

A

To add cape, cut here ↓

Fold

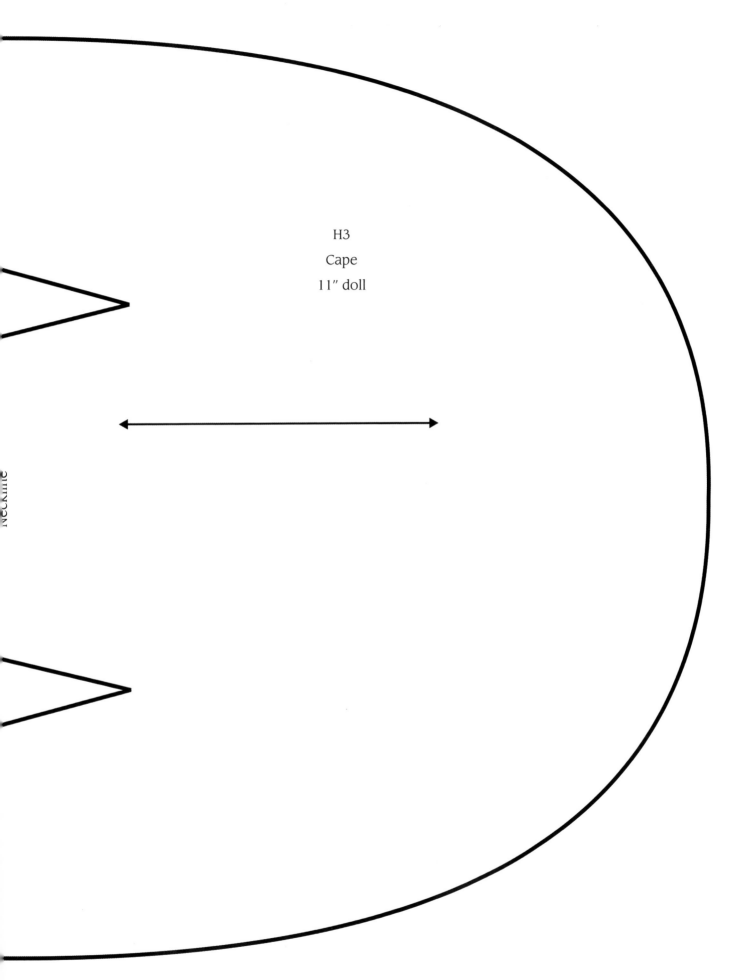

H3
Cape
11″ doll

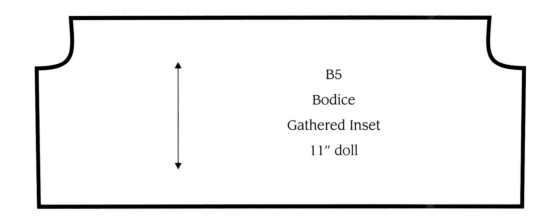

B5
Bodice
Gathered Inset
11″ doll

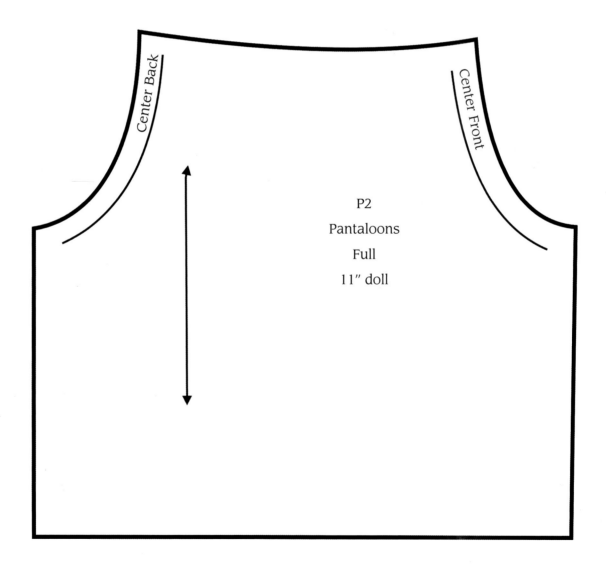

Center Back

Center Front

P2
Pantaloons
Full
11″ doll

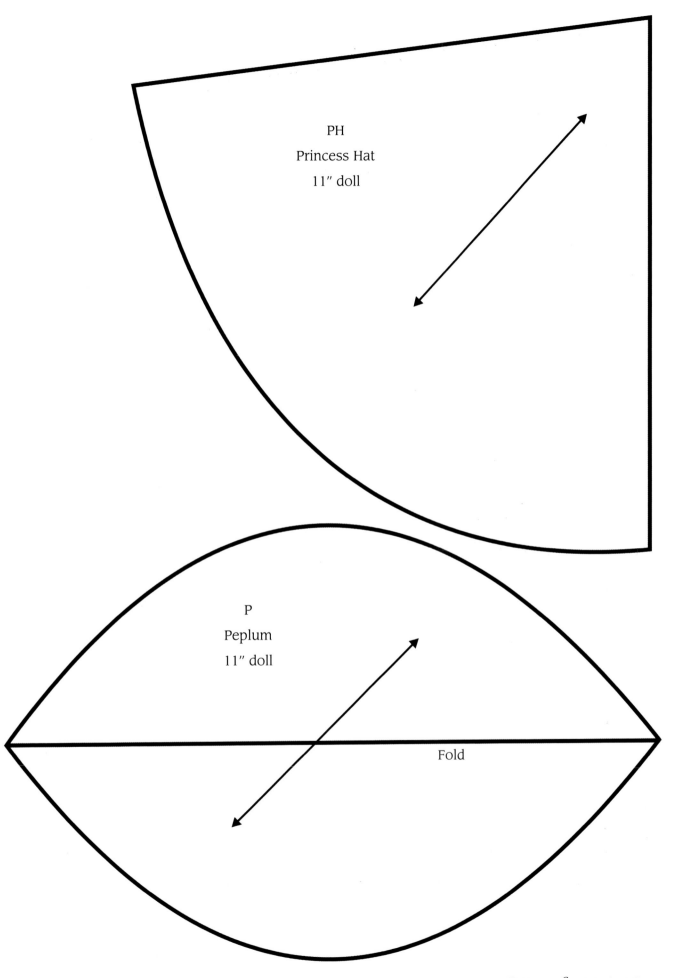

PH
Princess Hat
11″ doll

P
Peplum
11″ doll

Fold

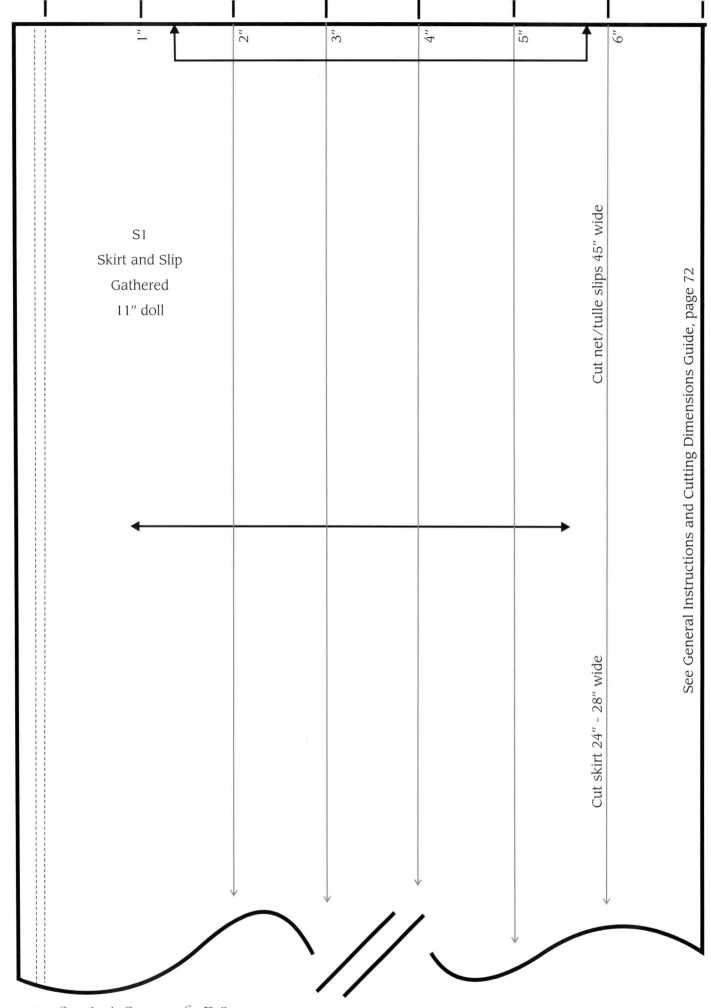

S1
Skirt and Slip
Gathered
11" doll

1" 2" 3" 4" 5" 6"

Cut net/tulle slips 45" wide

See General Instructions and Cutting Dimensions Guide, page 72

Cut skirt 24" - 28" wide

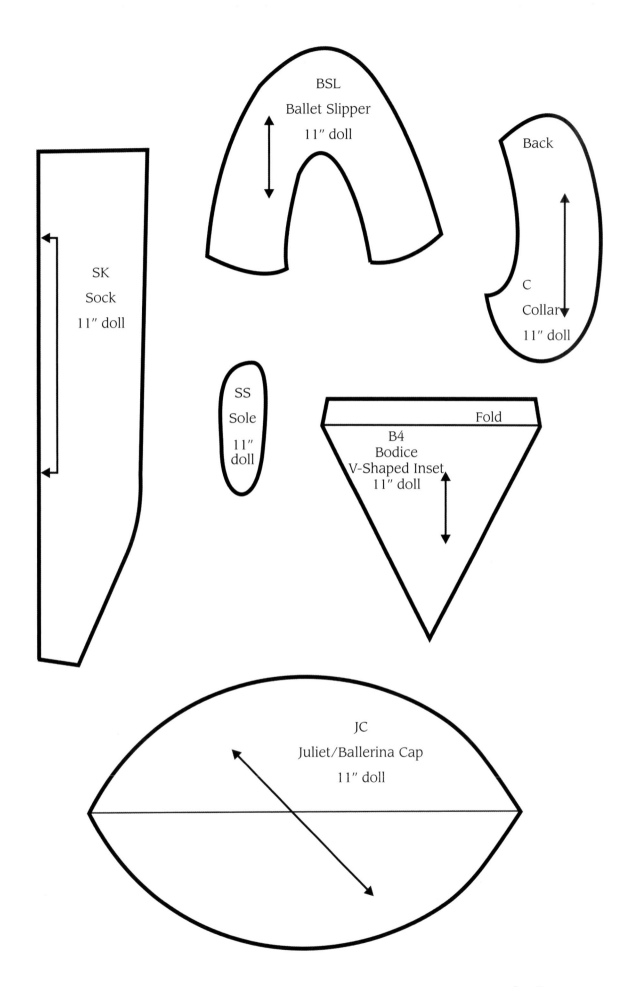

BSL
Ballet Slipper
11″ doll

Back

C
Collar
11″ doll

SK
Sock
11″ doll

SS
Sole
11″
doll

Fold

B4
Bodice
V-Shaped Inset
11″ doll

JC
Juliet/Ballerina Cap
11″ doll

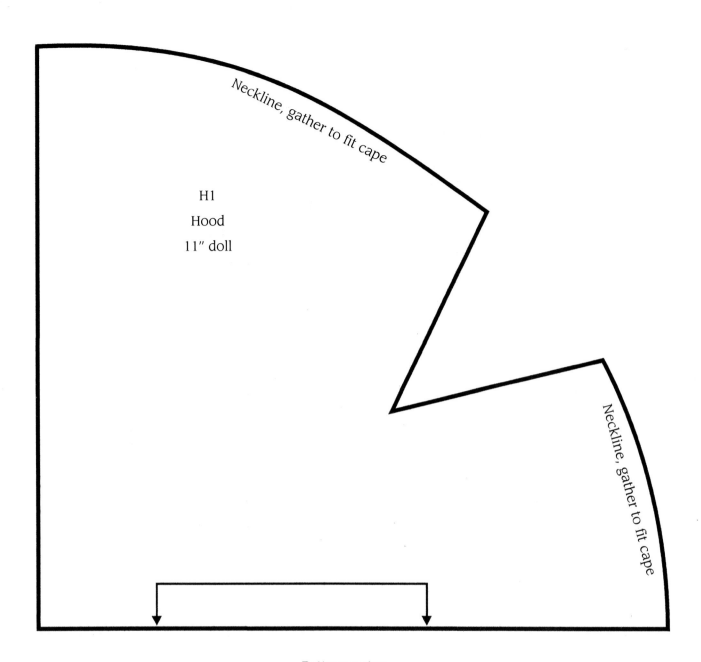

H1
Hood
11″ doll

Neckline, gather to fit cape

Neckline, gather to fit cape

Pattern notes

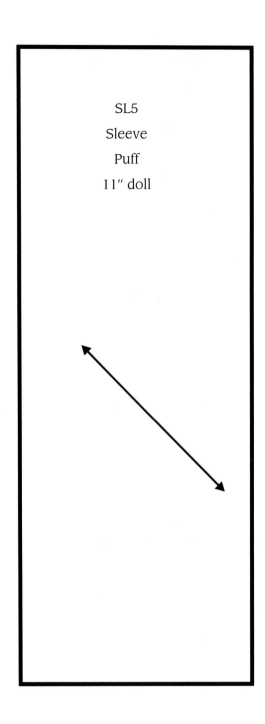

SL5
Sleeve
Puff
11″ doll

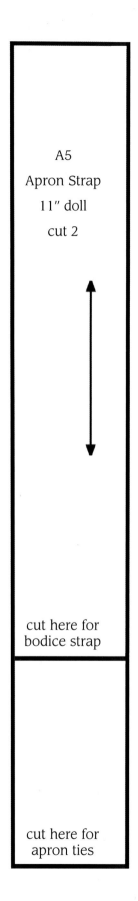

A5
Apron Strap
11″ doll
cut 2

cut here for
bodice strap

cut here for
apron ties

12-Inch Doll Patterns

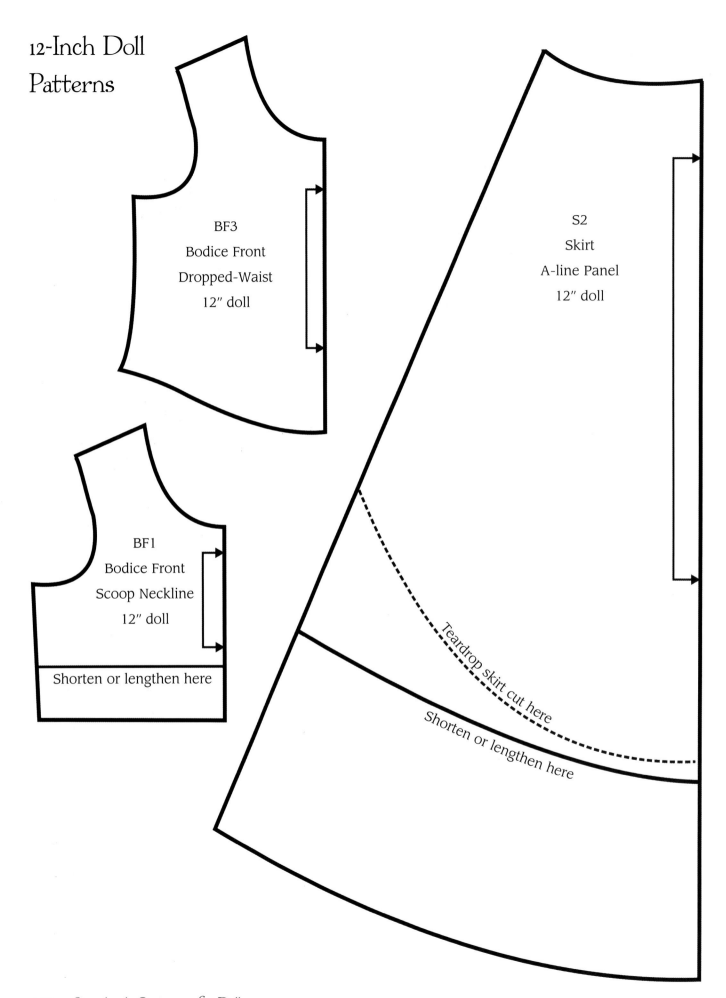

BF3
Bodice Front
Dropped-Waist
12″ doll

BF1
Bodice Front
Scoop Neckline
12″ doll

Shorten or lengthen here

S2
Skirt
A-line Panel
12″ doll

Teardrop skirt cut here

Shorten or lengthen here

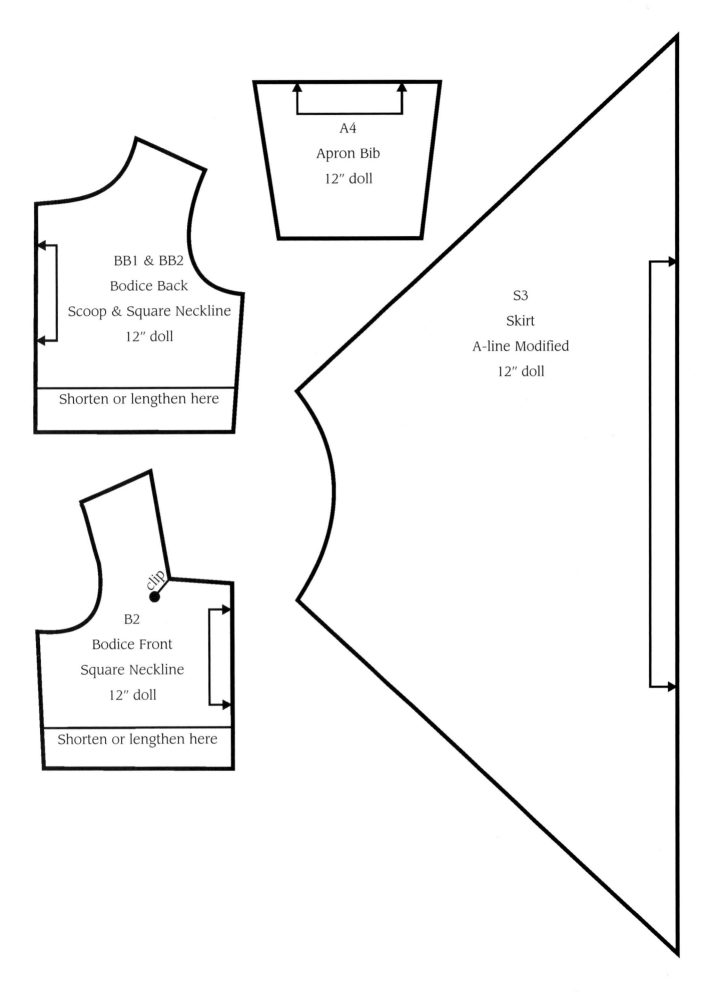

A4
Apron Bib
12" doll

BB1 & BB2
Bodice Back
Scoop & Square Neckline
12" doll

Shorten or lengthen here

B2
Bodice Front
Square Neckline
12" doll

Shorten or lengthen here

clip

S3
Skirt
A-line Modified
12" doll

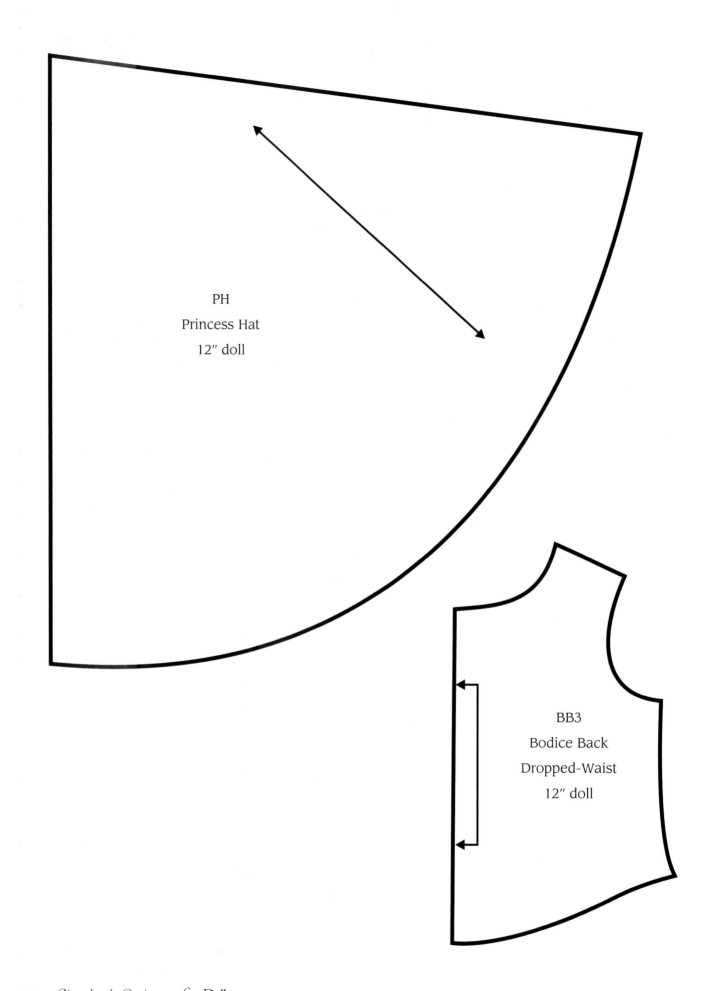

PH
Princess Hat
12″ doll

BB3
Bodice Back
Dropped-Waist
12″ doll

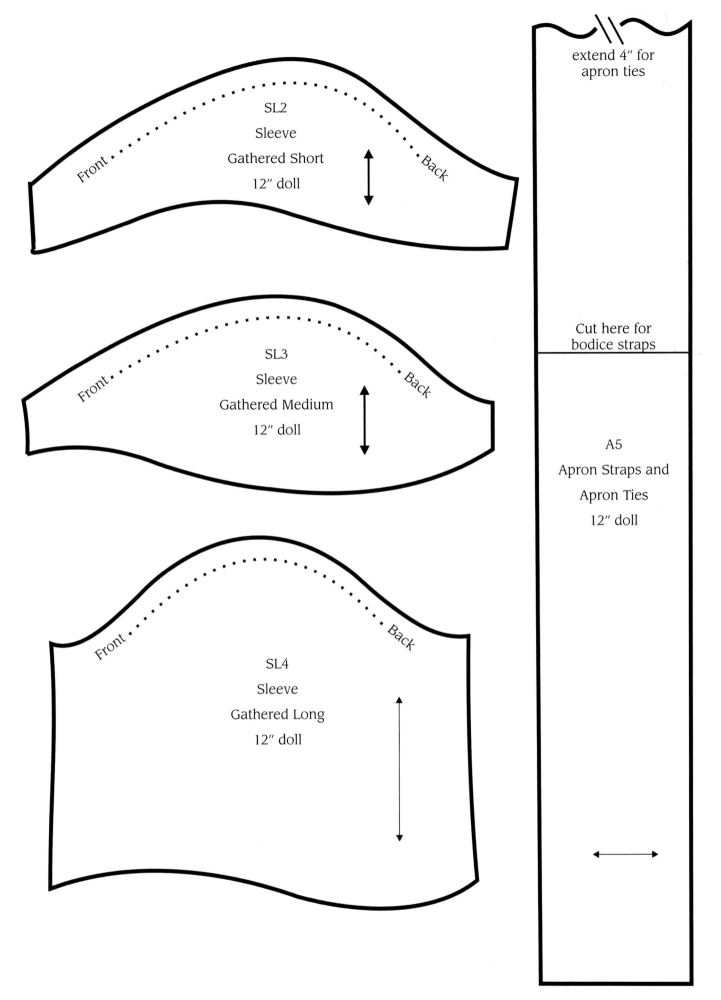

SL2
Sleeve
Gathered Short
12" doll

Front

Back

SL3
Sleeve
Gathered Medium
12" doll

Front

Back

SL4
Sleeve
Gathered Long
12" doll

Front

Back

extend 4" for
apron ties

Cut here for
bodice straps

A5
Apron Straps and
Apron Ties
12" doll

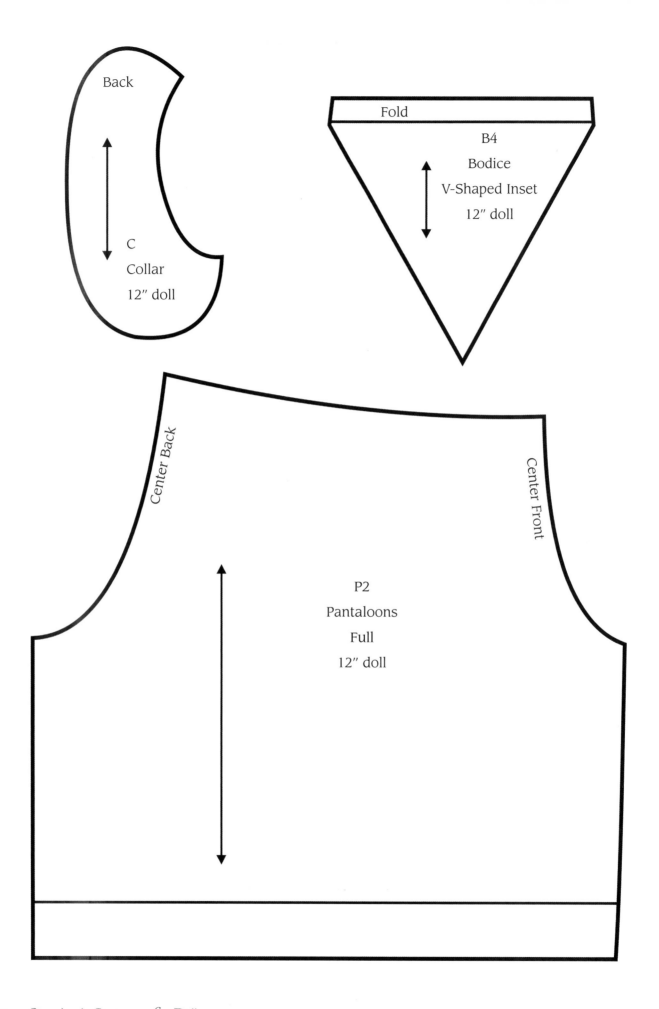

Back

C
Collar
12″ doll

Fold

B4
Bodice
V-Shaped Inset
12″ doll

Center Back

Center Front

P2
Pantaloons
Full
12″ doll

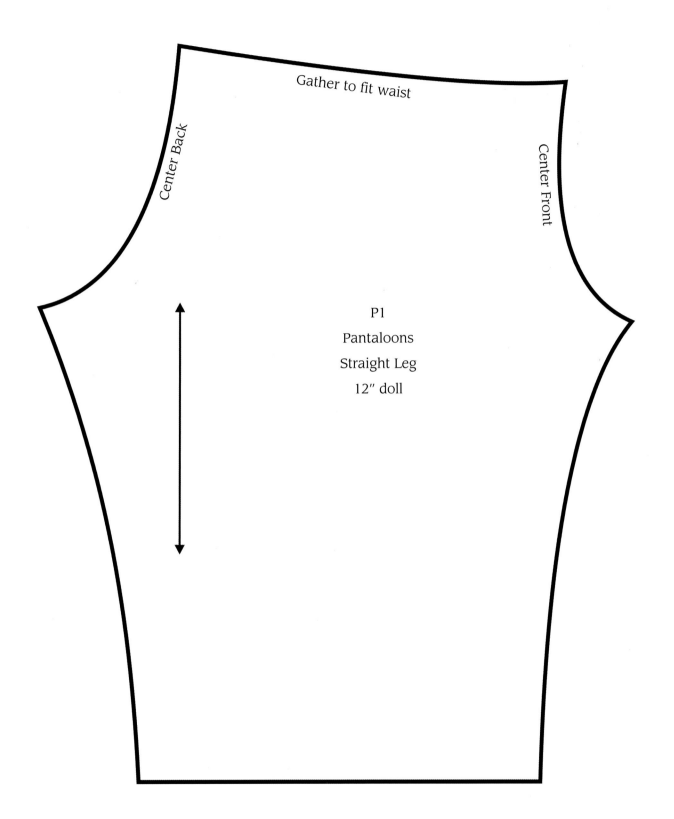

Gather to fit waist

Center Back

Center Front

P1
Pantaloons
Straight Leg
12″ doll

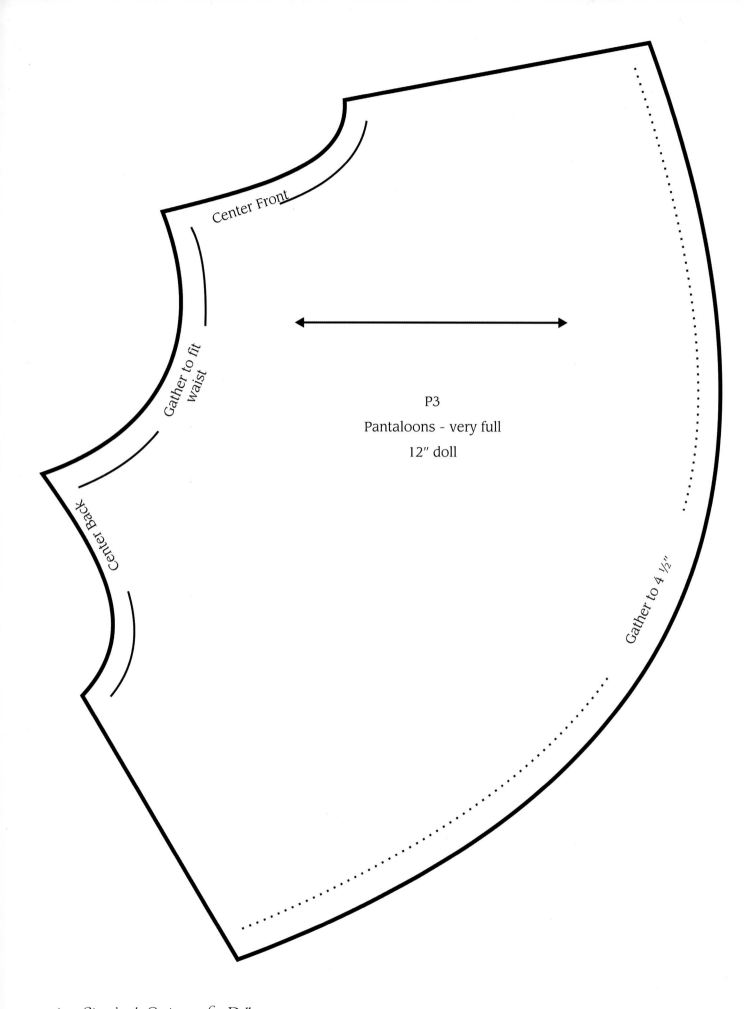

Center Front

Gather to fit waist

Center Back

P3
Pantaloons - very full
12″ doll

Gather to 4 ½″

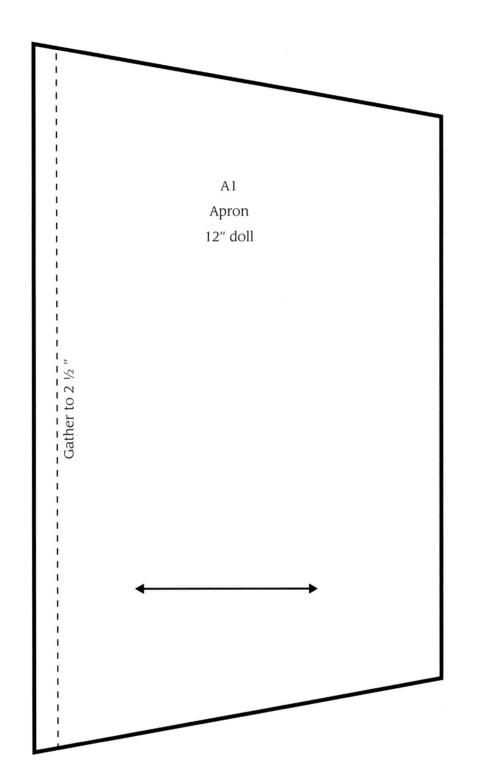

A1
Apron
12″ doll

Gather to 2 ½ ″

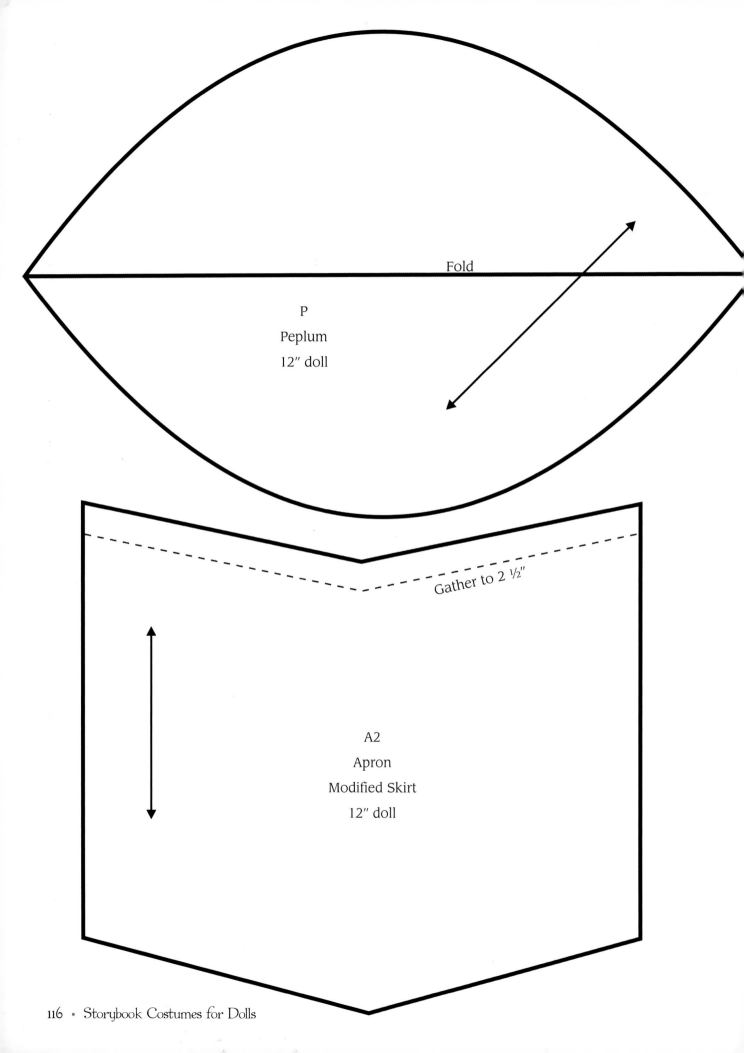

Fold

P
Peplum
12″ doll

Gather to 2 ½″

A2
Apron
Modified Skirt
12″ doll

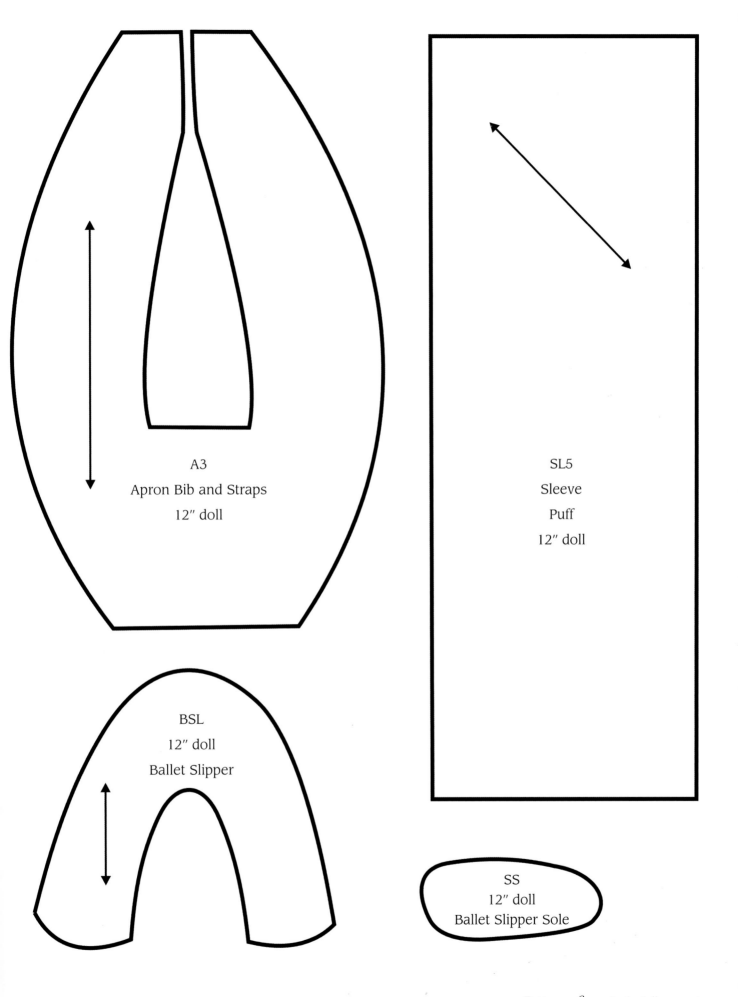

A3
Apron Bib and Straps
12″ doll

SL5
Sleeve
Puff
12″ doll

BSL
12″ doll
Ballet Slipper

SS
12″ doll
Ballet Slipper Sole

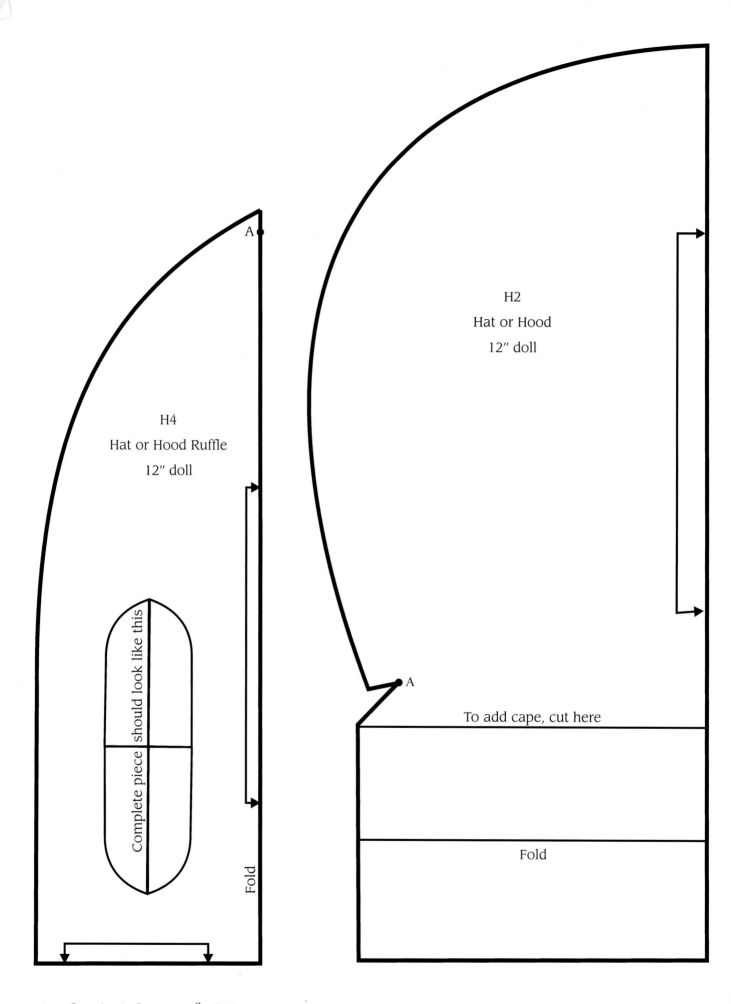

H4
Hat or Hood Ruffle
12″ doll

Complete piece should look like this

A

Fold

H2
Hat or Hood
12″ doll

A

To add cape, cut here

Fold

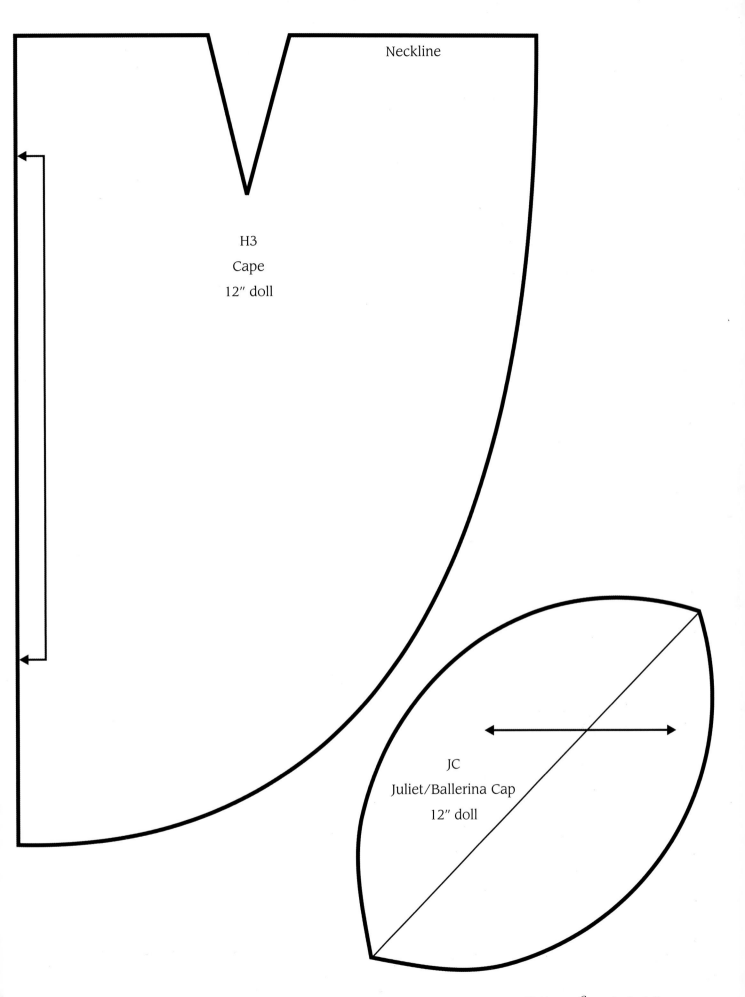

Neckline

H3
Cape
12″ doll

JC
Juliet/Ballerina Cap
12″ doll

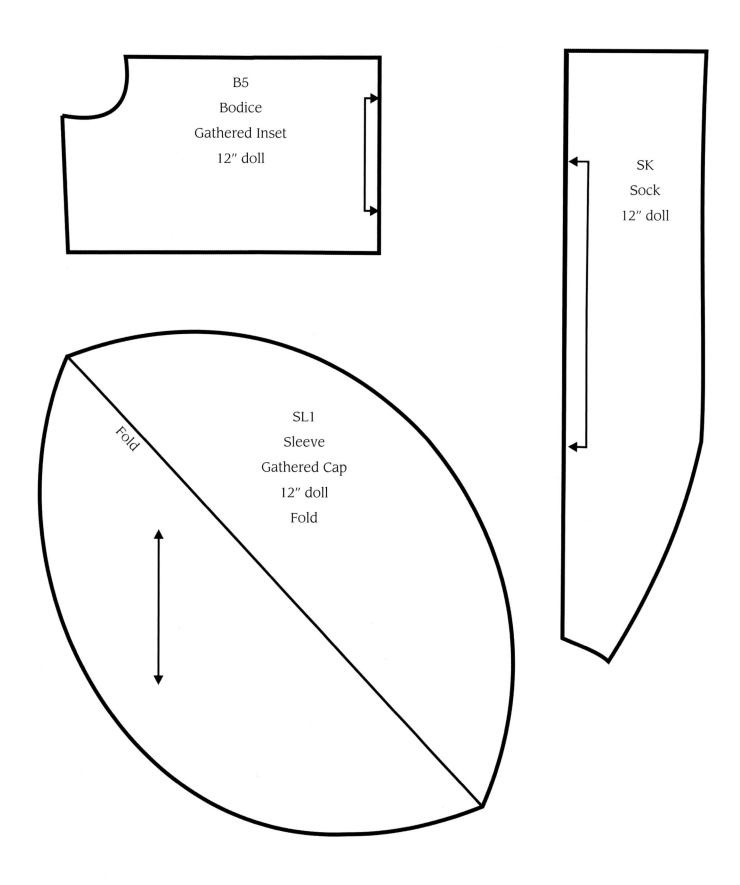

B5
Bodice
Gathered Inset
12″ doll

SK
Sock
12″ doll

SL1
Sleeve
Gathered Cap
12″ doll
Fold

Fold

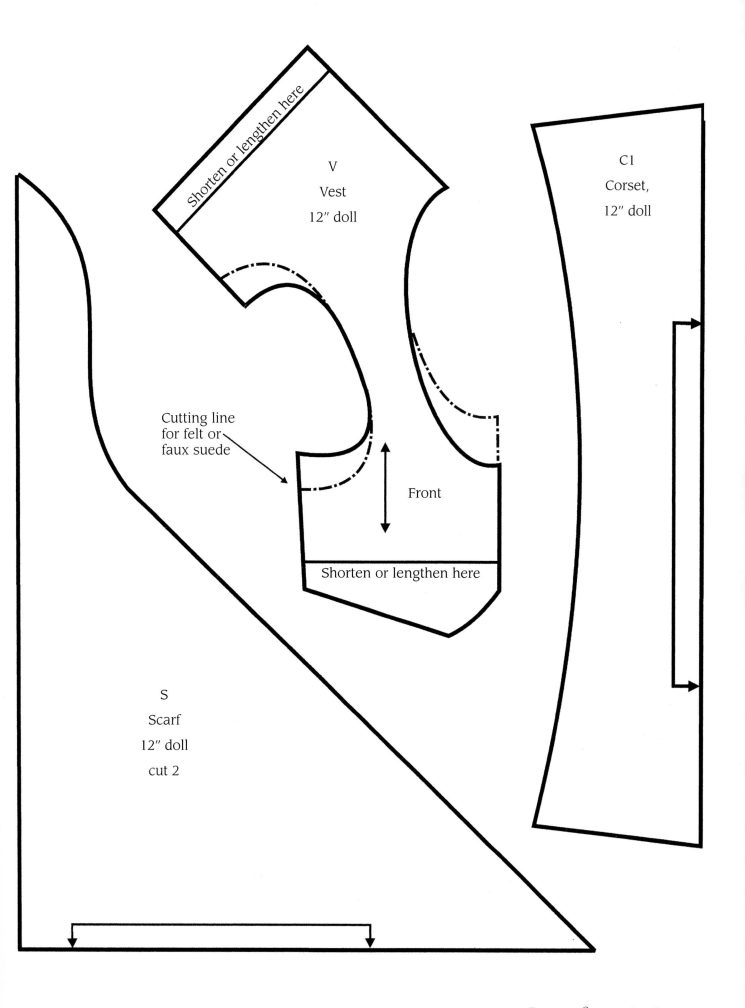

Shorten or lengthen here

V
Vest
12″ doll

C1
Corset,
12″ doll

Cutting line
for felt or
faux suede

Front

Shorten or lengthen here

S
Scarf
12″ doll
cut 2

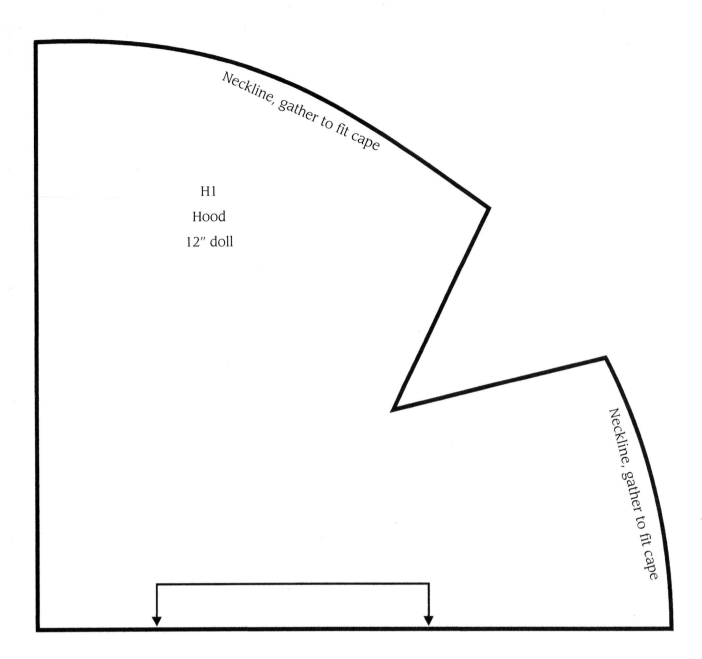

Neckline, gather to fit cape

H1
Hood
12″ doll

Neckline, gather to fit cape

Pattern notes

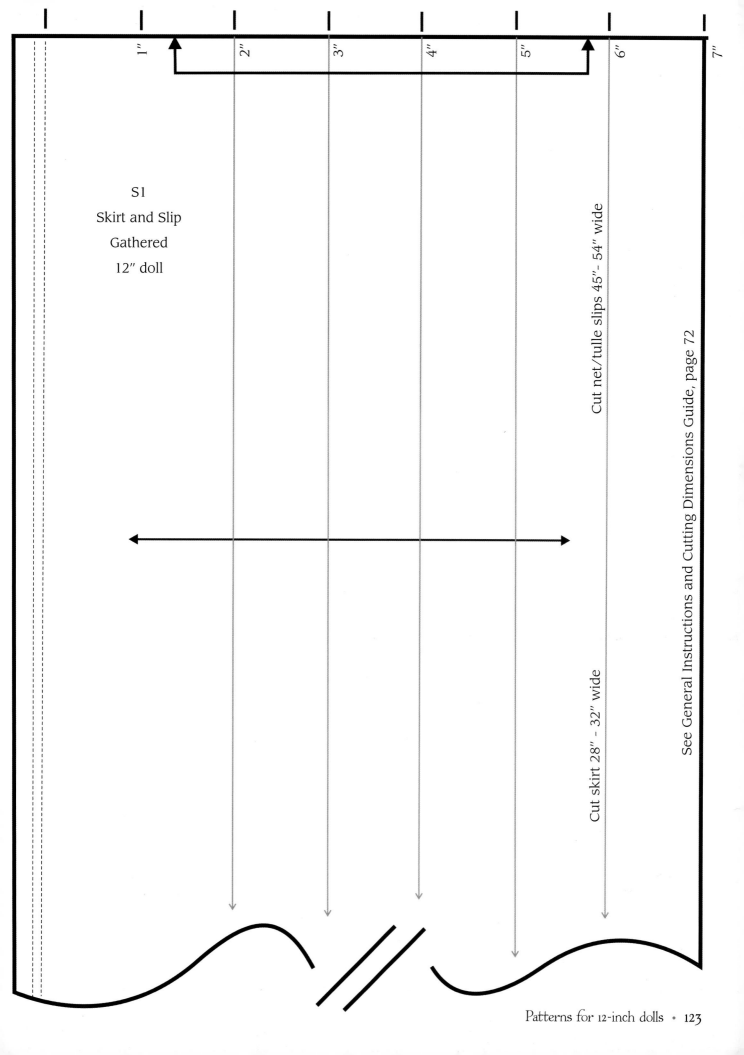

1" 2" 3" 4" 5" 6" 7"

S1
Skirt and Slip
Gathered
12″ doll

Cut net/tulle slips 45″– 54″ wide

See General Instructions and Cutting Dimensions Guide, page 72

Cut skirt 28″ – 32″ wide

Glossary

Basic bodice: In this book, a bodice front and back with lining attached at the neck and back edges; the bodice is turned and pressed, ready for the next step.

Basting stitch: Generally the longest machine stitch setting. It can be easily removed.

Bias: A line that run diagonally, at a 45° angle, across the weave of the fabric. The bias of the fabric has more stretch, allowing the fabric to drape with softer folds. Bias strips used for facings or casings are easier to fold and hem, especially around curves. Cut fabric to be used for piping on the bias of the fabric.

Doupioni (Douppioni): Fabric made from silk thread coming from two cocoons that have nested together. The thread is not separated in spinning, giving the yarn an uneven, irregular diameter.

Entre deux: The French term for insertion lace, referring to lace stitched between two fabrics or between fabric and trim or lace. Most often used in heirloom sewing, it is especially useful in doll costuming because of the fineness of the thread used and the narrow widths.

Facing: Fabric used to finish raw edges for a neat appearance.

Fray block product: Clear liquid product that dries quickly when applied to fabric. Used to prevent unraveling or to secure thread, it is more supple and less visible than glue.

Gathering stay: A strip of fabric, ribbon or cloth tape used to secure gathers. May be a visible trim or concealed, like a facing.

Gathering stitch: A sewing machine stitch that is longer than the regular seam stitching. Refer to the sewing machine manual for machine settings. Use this stitch to gather skirt, sleeve or pantaloon fabric. Gather the fabric by gently pulling the bobbin thread.

Hand: A textile term referring to the feel of the fabric—coarse versus smooth or silky—and how it drapes; for example, a brushed denim fabric may be smooth but stiff, while chiffon is fine with a soft drape.

Insertion lace: Narrow, straight-edged lace, often French loomed, used to stitch laces together. Intricate patterns add visual appeal.

Illusion: Lightweight netting, often used for wedding veils, 108 inches wide. Available in sparkle varieties.

A Real Princess, *as imagined by Katie McKain, barely eight years old*

Imagination: "The ability to form images or ideas in the mind, especially of things never seen or experienced directly."

—Microsoft Word

Point d'esprit: Originally, a light open stitch used in Guipure, a type of hand-made net or lace. Commonly referred to for netting with a dotted Swiss-type motif, with small points or dots stitched into the pattern; ideal for net stockings, slips, overlays, to add texture to the costume.

Serging: To finish a seam with a machine overlock stitch. A serged seam may be accomplished by using a serger, which is a sewing machine designed specifically for finishing fabric edges, or by using an overlock stitch on a universal sewing machine.

Silk embroidery ribbon: Very fine silk ribbon, generally 2mm-6mm wide, excellent for tiny bows or ribbon roses, it is also available in man-made fibers.

Stabilizer: Used to stabilize fabric while stitching. Available in water soluble, tear away and in varying weights, by the yard or packaged. Recommended for stitching on small pieces or light-weight fabrics.

Taffeta: A fine plain-weave fabric, generally with sheen. There are different weights and weaves. Those that fray easily may not be suitable for doll clothing.

Tulle: Fine, very lightweight, machine-made inexpensive net. Available in plain, sparkle and glitter varieties.

Water-soluble marker: Felt-tipped marker designed to write on fabric. Ink disappears when water is applied. (Test a fabric swatch before use, especially on fine fabrics.)

Bibliography

Andersen, Hans Christian. *The Princess and the Pea*. Denmark: C. A. Reitzel, 1835.

Boucher, François, *20,000 Years of Fashion, The History of Costume and Personal Adornment*. New York: Harry N. Abrams, Inc, 1966.

Carroll, Lewis. *Alice's Adventures in Wonderland*. U.S.A.: Grolier Classics, Grolier Incorporated, 1956.

Carroll, Lewis. *The Nursery Alice*. England: Macmillan, 1890.

Caulfeild, Sophia Francs Anne and Blanche C. Saward. *The Dictionary of Needlework*, Facsimile of the 1882 Edition. New York: Arno Press, 1972.

Dan River. *A Dictionary of Textile Terms*. Danville, Virginia: Dan River Inc., 1971.

Grimm, Jacob and Wilhelm. *Snow White*. Berlin: 1812. Translated by Robert Godwin-Jones, Virginia Commonwealth University, Department of Foreign Languages, 2008.

Hoffmann, E.T.A. *Nutcracker,* New York: Crown Publishing Group, 1984.

Hoffmann, E.T.A. *The Nutcracker and the Mouse King*. Wikipedia®, GNU Free Documentation License, 2008.

Perrault, Charles. "Little Red Riding Hood." *Tales of Mother Goose*. Wikpedia®, GNU Free Documentation License, 2008.

Shakespeare, William. *Romeo and Juliet*. Wikipedia®, GNU Free Documentation License, 2008.

Spyri, Johanna. *Heidi*. U.S.A.: Harper Festival®, a division of Harper Collins Publishers, New York, NY, 2006.

Tulah as an Avant Garde Real Princess

Illustration Credits

Doré, Gustave. "Little Red Riding Hood." *Les Contes de Perrault*, 1867. Wikimedia Commons. Contributed by Thuresson, 2006. Public Domain.

Dulac, Edmund. "Princess and Pea." *Stories from Hans Andersen*, London: Hodder & Stoughton, Ltd. 1911. Wikipedia Commons. Contributed by Bryan Bot. 2007. GNU Free Documentation License.

Ford, A.J. "A True Princess." 1894. Wikipedia Commons. Contributed by LaSylphide, 2008. GNU Free Documentation License.

Gustafson, Scott. "Little Bo Peep" ©1990. All rights reserved. *Favorite Nursery Rhymes from Mother Goose.* Seymour, Connecticut: Greenwich Workshop Press, 2007.

Jüttner, Franz. "Snow White." *Schneewittchen*, 1910. Mainz: Scholz' Künstler-Bilderbücher. Wikimedia Commons. 2008. Public Domain.

Münger, Rudolf. "Heidi." *Heidi,* 1880. Wikimedia Commons. Contributed by Adrian Michael, 2006. GNU Free Documentation License.

Tenniel, John. "Alice Managing her Flamingo" and "Alice, Drink Me." *Alice's Adventures in Wonderland*, 1865. U.S.A.: Grolier Classics, Grolier Incorporated, 1956.

Vzevolozhsky, Ivan. "For Dance with Little Fifes." Original sketch for *The Nutcracker* ballet, 1892. Wikipedia Commons.

Waterhouse, John William. "Juliet or The Blue Necklace." 1898. Wikimedia Commons. Contributed by Fleance. 2006. GNU Free Documentation License.

Watts, George Frederic. "Little Red Riding Hood." 1890. Wikimedia Commons. Project Gutenberg eText 17395.jpg . *The Book of Art for Young People.* Agnes Conway, Sir Martin Conway. Public Domain.

Ginny as an Old World Real Princess

About the Author

Londie Phillips graduated from San Francisco School of Fashion Design in 1973 and worked in various design fields while raising her family. In 1993, she entered the world of dolls. As a designer for Ashton Drake Galleries, she dressed many licensed doll editions including: Madame Alexander®, Precious Moments®, Berta Hummel®, Thomas Kinkade®, Swarovski®, Gene®, © Warner Brothers and © Disney. In collaboration with doll artist Dianna Effner, Londie's designs have been sold world wide, dressing DOTY® Award winners and nominees, and limited-edition and one-of-a-kind art dolls. They have also been showcased at National Institute of American Doll Artists (NIADA) group exhibitions. She is the exclusive designer for Nancy Ann Storybook Doll Company® and also designs for © Charisma Brands. Her how-to articles and patterns have appeared in *Sew News*, *Doll Crafter* and for *Expressions*.

"Whatever your hand finds to do, do it with all your might"
—King Solomon, Ecclesiastes 9:10 NIV